WALKER PERCY

Modern Critical Views

These and other titles in preparation

Modern Critical Views

WALKER PERCY

Edited and with an introduction by
Harold Bloom
Sterling Professor of the Humanities
Yale University

CHELSEA HOUSE PUBLISHERS ◊ 1986
New York ◊ New Haven ◊ Philadelphia

© 1986 by Chelsea House Publishers, a division of Chelsea
House Educational Communications, Inc.
   133 Christopher Street, New York, NY 10014
   345 Whitney Avenue, New Haven, CT 06511
   5014 West Chester Pike, Edgemont, PA 19028

Introduction © 1986 by Harold Bloom

Printed and bound in the United States of America

∞ The paper used in this publication meets the minimum
requirements of the American National Standard for Permanence
of Paper for Printed Library Materials, Z39.48–1984.

Library of Congress Cataloging-in-Publication Data
Walker Percy.
   (Modern critical views)
   Bibliography: p.
   Includes index.
   1. Percy, Walker, 1916–   —Criticism and interpretation.
I. Bloom, Harold, 1930–   II. Series.
PS3566.E6912Z94   1986   813'.54   86–6838
ISBN 0–87754–714–9 (alk. paper)

Contents

Editor's Note

This book gathers together the best criticism yet published upon the novels of Walker Percy, the contemporary American Southern novelist. The essays are arranged here in the chronological order of their original publication. I am grateful to Henry Finder for his customary erudition and judgment in locating and helping to choose much of this criticism.

My introduction offers a reading of Percy's first novel, *The Moviegoer*, which I continue to prefer to his four subsequent major fictions. Tony Tanner's analysis of *The Moviegoer* provides a very different perspective, since my remarks are elegiac in regard to Percy's development from spiritual ruefulness to a prophetic moralism that rivals Jeremiah's in its poignant intensity. Tanner's portrait of Percy's moviegoer as an "alienated wonderer" shrewdly relates Binx Bolling to that long tradition moving between Melville's Ishmael and Scott Fitzgerald's Nick Carraway.

Reviewing *The Last Gentleman*, Percy's transitional novel towards his prophetic concerns, Frederick C. Crews locates what he judges to be a lack of "emotional substance" in Percy's representation of his hero, Will Barrett. *Love in the Ruins* is exuberantly read by Martin Luschei as a seriocomic masterpiece, somehow overcoming alienation, a judgment that strikes me as generous and disputable. Yet more disputable, intentionally so, is the fiercely polemical essay by the distinguished critic Cleanth Brooks, who reads Percy as sharing in Eric Voegelin's massive crusade against modern gnosticism. Doubtless, Brooks is imaginatively accurate, though Percy, like ancient Christianity itself, seems to me deeply contaminated by the gnosticism that he and Brooks and Voegelin so eloquently oppose.

A powerful contemporary, the novelist Joyce Carol Oates, reviews Percy's *Lancelot* with a countereloquence that rejects the novel as a confusion of tones and an uncontrolled mixture of genres. Returning to *The Last Gentleman*, Richard Pindell movingly defends the book's open-endedness as "a gesture of hope." A third perspective upon the novel is then given by

Simone Vauthier, who unlike Crews, and even Pindell, discovers authentic profundity in its "manipulation of the narrative triangle," since that manipulation compels us to meditate afresh upon "the relationship between words and things and people and being."

In a return to *Lancelot,* the Romantic scholar Jerome C. Christensen does not argue against a negative judgment like that of Joyce Carol Oates, but instead moves the grounds of argument by suggesting: "Fiction and tract, narrative and harangue, *Lancelot* is a book that collapses under the pressure of its message." What seems to me an even more problematic novel, *The Second Coming,* is analyzed by Doreen A. Fowler as a book in which Percy, despite his overt intentions, fails to deliver answers, not because of the novel's ambiguity but because of its continued ambivalence.

In a synoptic consideration, Patricia Lewis Poteat ends this volume with an intricate essay on Percy as storyteller, contrasting three of his novels and two of his essays. Her conclusions ought to be compared with those of my introduction, since she sees more continuity in Percy's storytelling art than I can, though she too expresses an anxiety as to whether Percy the novelist can withstand Percy the moral and religious prophet, and Percy the philosophical essayist.

Introduction

With many other readers, I discovered *The Moviegoer* in 1961, and was delighted. Rereading it a quarter-century later, the delight returns, but perhaps somewhat darkened by intimations in the novel of the moral and religious obsessions that have made each subsequent fiction by Walker Percy rather more problematic than the one before. As a storyteller, Percy chooses to follow the downward path to wisdom, perhaps at the expense of his stories. *The Last Gentleman* (1966) had not abandoned all the narrative concerns of *The Moviegoer,* but *Love in the Ruins* (1971) resorts to apocalyptic yearnings, and *Lancelot* (1977) seems to address a saving remnant. *The Second Coming* (1980) is a wholly tendentious narrative and hardly seems to be by the author of *The Moviegoer.* Acclaimed as a Southern prophet, Percy may have become precisely that. There is a curious progression in his novels' closing passages that is revelatory of a metamorphosis from the language of story to the urgencies that transcend art:

> I watch her walk toward St. Charles, cape jasmine held against her cheek, until my brothers and sisters call out behind me.
>
> (The Moviegoer)

> "Wait," he shouted in a dead run. The Edsel paused, sighed, and stopped. Strength flowed like oil into his muscles and he ran with great joyous ten-foot antelope bounds. The Edsel waited for him.
>
> (The Last Gentleman)

> To bed we go for a long winter's nap, twined about each other as the ivy twineth not under a bush or in a car or on the floor

or any such humbug as marked the past peculiar years of Christendom, but at home in bed where all good folk belong.

(Love in the Ruins)

Do you know her well?
Yes.
Will she join me in Virginia and will she and I and Siobhan begin a new life there?
Yes.
Very well. I've finished. Is there anything you wish to tell me before I leave?
Yes.

(Lancelot)

His heart leapt with a secret joy. What is it I want from her and him, he wondered, not only want but must have? Is she a gift and therefore a sign of a giver? Could it be that the Lord is here, masquerading behind this simple silly holy face? Am I crazy to want both, her and Him? No, not want, must have. And will have.

(The Second Coming)

Even out of context, Percy's conclusions move him and his readers from a narrative poignance to a theocentric anxiety. It cannot be gratuitous that both *Lancelot* and *The Second Coming* end with the hero conversing with a kindly priest. "The past peculiar years of Christendom" craze Percy's protagonists, and by implication Percy thinks the worse of us for not being so crazed. Despite the manifest humor of his *Lost in the Cosmos: The Last Self-Help Book* (1983), Percy intends its conclusion as what can only be called a low seriousness:

Repeat. Do you read? Do you read? Are you in trouble? How did you get in trouble? If you are in trouble, have you sought help? If you did, did help come? If it did, did you accept it? Are you out of trouble? What is the character of your consciousness? Are you conscious? Do you have a self? Do you know who you are? Do you know what you are doing? Do you love? Do you know how to love? Are you loved? Do you hate? Do you read me? Come back. Repeat. Come back. Come back. Come back.

(CHECK ONE)

II

A rereading of *The Moviegoer* after a first reading of *Lancelot* and *The Second Coming* must confront a critic with a bemused sense of loss. Binx Bolling is more than the most amiable of Percy's surrogates; his freedom from the drive to moralize has about it now the aura of his author's lost freedom. Aunt Emily, the book's moralizer, is a presage of many a Percyan denunciation to come, and yet her highly individual style allows us to absorb her condemnations as we cannot quite sustain the scoldings that come in Percy's later novels:

> Our civilization has achieved a distinction of sorts. It will be remembered not for its technology nor even its wars but for its novel ethos. Ours is the only civilization in history which has enshrined mediocrity as its national ideal. Others have been corrupt, but leave it to us to invent the most undistinguished of corruptions. No orgies, no blood running in the street, no babies thrown off cliffs. No, we're sentimental people and we horrify easily. True, our moral fiber is rotten. Our national character stinks to high heaven. But we are kinder than ever. No prostitute ever responded with a quicker spasm of sentiment when our hearts are touched. Nor is there anything new about thievery, lewdness, lying, adultery. What is new is that in our time liars and thieves and whores and adulterers wish also to be congratulated and are congratulated by the great public, if their confession is sufficiently psychological or strikes a sufficiently heartfelt and authentic note of sincerity.

However much we admire the formidable Aunt Emily and rightly find this rhetoric to be suitable to her, none among us could regard this as what is best or most enduring in *The Moviegoer*. Binx is just that; he is a kind of grown-up, ruefully respectable New Orleans version of Twain's Huckleberry Finn. Like Huck, Binx longs for freedom while fearing solitude. But an Existentialist Huck Finn is a sublime joke, and this joke still seems to me Percy's authentic and very considerable achievement. *The Moviegoer* alone of Percy's fictions, to date, is a permanent American book. If that judgment is right, then the waste of Percy's authentic talents is a lamentable instance of art yielding to moralism, of storytelling subverted by religious nostalgias.

I remember how much I initially liked *The Moviegoer*'s first paragraph, and am very fond of it still:

> This morning I got a note from my aunt asking me to come for

lunch. I know what this means. Since I go there every Sunday for dinner and today is Wednesday, it can mean only one thing: she wants to have one of her serious talks. It will be extremely grave, either a piece of bad news about her stepdaughter Kate or else a serious talk about me, about the future and what I ought to do. It is enough to scare the wits out of anyone, yet I confess I do not find the prospect altogether unpleasant.

The whole of the book is subtly present in this beginning, since Kate's suicidal despairs are the dark center of the moviegoer's life as a man, to borrow Philip Roth's foreboding phrase. Present also is the antithetical strain in Binx Bolling, who finds reality in his aunt's moral stance, without however being able to erase the distance that divides him from it, and from every other conceivable position. Yet Binx, as he reveals to us very early, is nothing but a quester, who seeks what everyone else asserts they have found:

> What do you seek—God? you ask with a smile.
> I hesitate to answer, since all other Americans have settled the matter for themselves and to give such an answer would amount to setting myself a goal which everyone else has reached—and therefore raising a question in which no one has the slightest interest. Who wants to be dead last among one hundred and eighty million Americans? For, as everyone knows, the polls report that 98% of Americans believe in God and the remaining 2% are atheists and agnostics—which leaves not a single percentage point for a seeker. For myself, I enjoy answering polls as much as anyone and take pleasure in giving intelligent replies to all questions.
> Truthfully, it is the fear of exposing my own ignorance which constrains me from mentioning the object of my search. For, to begin with, I cannot even answer this, the simplest and most basic of all questions: Am I, in my search, a hundred miles ahead of my fellow Americans or a hundred miles behind them? That is to say: Have 98% of Americans already found what I seek or are they so sunk in everydayness that not even the possibility of a search has occurred to them?
> On my honor, I do not know the answer.

Binx clearly would not have written *Lancelot, The Second Coming,* and *Lost in the Cosmos,* but then neither would Kate, nor even Aunt Emily, whose realistic sense of cultural and societal crisis eschews violence, even rhetorical violence, as a response. When she impressively observes that "it should be quite a sight, the going under of the evening land," Binx thinks, "For her too the fabric is dissolving, but for her even the dissolving makes sense." That may be the difference between Aunt Emily and the later Percy; if for you even the dissolving makes sense, then your response will be wholly coherent, and you will be saved from responding to violence with violence.

Binx, as the moviegoer, has become a quietist, who neither judges nor can be judged. His bond with Kate is that both seek "certification" in his special sense:

> Afterwards in the street, she looks around the neighborhood. "Yes, it is certified now."
> She refers to a phenomenon of moviegoing which I have called certification. Nowadays when a person lives somewhere, in a neighborhood, the place is not certified for him. More than likely he will live there sadly and the emptiness which is inside him will expand until it evacuates the entire neighborhood. But if he sees a movie which shows his very neighborhood, it becomes possible for him to live, for a time at least, as a person who is Somewhere and not Anywhere.

This, in a touchingly minimal way, is somehow to be provisionally redeemed by representation, which no longer augments the self, as it did for Walt Whitman, but at least keeps one's context from becoming totally emptied out. Binx and Kate win our affection, as no one subsequently in Percy can. Doubtless, Percy did not care to give us such charming protagonists in his later novels, precisely because they subvert his prophetic concerns. Still, it seems not wrong to hope that the novelist might yet return to his gentler and more qualified visions.

III

Walker Percy is scarcely alone in attempting to employ the novel as a spiritual weapon against the malaise of the age. He is not even unique in combining an apocalyptic temperament with Roman Catholicism, though *Lancelot* does not match Flannery O'Connor in that odd blend. Yet he does have a singular predilection for moral theology, and at times achieves a curious authority in his uncanny mode. With a stance very different from that of Protestant Fundamentalists, he regards the Jews as the eternal evidence for the reality of Yahweh, and the historical authenticity of the Roman Catholic Church. Like most of the Jewish people, I am normally rather wary

of such a search for evidences, but Percy handles it with tact and humane
wit, benign if a little unnerving. In *The Moviegoer,* Binx identifies his own,
internal exile with that of the Jews:

> An odd thing. Ever since Wednesday I have become acutely aware
> of Jews. There is a clue here, but of what I cannot say. How do
> I know? Because whenever I approach a Jew, the Geiger counter
> in my head starts rattling away like a machine gun; and as I go
> past with the utmost circumspection and with every sense alert—
> the Geiger counter subsides.
>
> There is nothing new in my Jewish vibrations. During the years
> when I had friends my Aunt Edna, who is a theosophist, noticed
> that all my friends were Jews. She knew why moreover: I had
> been a Jew in a previous incarnation. Perhaps that is it. Anyhow
> it is true that I am Jewish by instinct. We share the same exile.
> The fact is, however, I am more Jewish than the Jews I know.
> They are more at home than I am. I accept my exile.
>
> Another evidence of my Jewishness: the other day a sociologist
> reported that a significantly large percentage of solitary movie-
> goers are Jews.
>
> Jews are my first real clue.
>
> When a man is in despair and does not in his heart of hearts
> allow that a search is possible and when such a man passes a Jew
> in the street, he notices nothing.
>
> When a man becomes a scientist or an artist, he is open to a
> different kind of despair. When such a man passes a Jew in the
> street, he may notice something but it is not a remarkable en-
> counter. To him the Jew can only appear as a scientist or artist
> like himself or as a specimen to be studied.
>
> But when a man awakes to the possibility of a search and when
> such a man passes a Jew in the street for the first time, he is like
> Robinson Crusoe seeing the footprint on the beach.

The wit of assimilating the Jewish Sabbath, which begins at sundown
on Friday, to the trace of Defoe's Friday, conceals the moral intensity of the
passage. Miraculously surviving, the Jews are the searcher's prime mark or
sign of the promise of God that cannot be voided. The culmination of this
sign in Percy is Will Barrett's humorous but obsessive concern with the
supposed absence or flight of Jews from North Carolina in *The Second
Coming.* Barrett's equivocal madness keeps returning him to the Jews as a
sign, particularly in an extraordinary letter that he writes:

To be specific: I wish you to monitor the demographic movement of Jews not only from North Carolina but from other states and other countries as well, to take note of any extraordinary changes which go contrary to established demographic patterns— such as the emigration of blacks from the South (and their present return). If, for example, there has occurred or should occur a massive exodus of Jews from the U.S. to Israel, I request that you establish an observation post in the village of Megiddo in the narrow waist of Israel (the site, as you may know, of ancient Armageddon), where a foe from the east would logically attempt to cut Israel in two. From this point you can monitor any unusual events in the Arab countries to the east, particularly the emergence of a leader of extraordinary abilities—another putative sign of the last days.

The saving difference between this madness, and the somber stuff I hear from television evangelists every night, is that Barrett is only mad north-northwest, and Percy's apocalyptic wind is blowing at us from the south. Still in midcareer, the author of *The Moviegoer* may yet cease searching for signs, and instead return to his gift for ruefully comic narrative. As a critic, I want to approach Walker Percy while waving a banner before me: "Bring back Binx Bolling!"

TONY TANNER

The Moviegoer *and American Fiction:* Wonder and Alienation

In mentioning Walker Percy's *The Moviegoer* my aim is not to extol an undiscovered masterpiece but simply to take a recent, talented first novel and show how unmistakably it relates itself to the lines of development we have discussed [previously]. Binx Bolling, the narrator, is a sort of American Outsider. But the manner of his rebellion and the form of his alienation differ from those of his French counterpart. His desire is to preserve a sense of wonder: his dread is the feeling of being "cut loose metaphysically speaking" (very much as Hemingway dreaded *nada* and Sherwood Anderson shivered to feel that all life might simply be "a vastness and emptiness"). He aspires to find some sort of lodgement and anchorage in the world without inwardly capitulating to the false standards and dead values and empty gestures of the world's inhabitants, even though outwardly, as we shall see, he is quite willing to imitate them, to appear as one of the herd. His sense of alienation is often brought out in the manner in which he describes other people, people who are utterly and complacently at home in the world, people who, to use Anderson's phrase, have "no sense of strangeness, no wonder about life." For example, the dull efficient businessman, Eddie Lovell who looks out on the world and sees no mystery. "He understands everything out there and everything out there is something to be understood." The accurate yet utterly detached, cool way in which he describes such people is reminiscent of the strategy by Camus in *L'Étranger* of which Sartre very shrewdly said:

From *The Reign of Wonder: Naivety and Reality in American Literature.* © 1965 by Cambridge University Press. Originally entitled "Afterword: Wonder and Alienation—The Mystic and the Moviegoer."

M. Camus has a method ready to hand. He is going to insert a glass partition between the reader and his characters. Is there anything sillier than a man behind a glass window? Glass seems to let everything through. It stops only one thing: the meaning of his gestures. The glass remains to be chosen. It will be the Outsider's mind, which is really transparent, since we see everything it sees. However, it is so constructed as to be transparent to things and opaque to meanings.

(One might add that a child's mind is often "transparent to things and opaque to meanings" and it is not surprising that the child has so often been employed in recent fiction as a vehicle for a sense of alienation).

Percy's narrator, to all outward appearances utterly normal and conventional, moves through society feeling like a Jew. "We share the same exile. The fact is, however, I am more Jewish than the Jews I know. They are more at home than I am. I accept my exile." (Norman Mailer has given us the white negro, now we have the gentile Jew.) He laughs and talks with people as occasion demands, but "all the friendly and likable people seem dead to me; only the haters seem alive." (A conclusion Salinger shied away from.) Even as he describes, without acrid comment, the nice people he meets, we see them as corpses through the cold glass of his mind. Only with his cousin Kate does he feel real sympathy, and she is in the process of having a nervous breakdown not dissimilar to Franny [Glass's] since she too feels that everything is "so—no 'count, somehow." When, at the end of the book, Binx's aunt arraigns him in the name of all the traditional values and virtues of which she herself is a dignified upholder he can only remain silent. He does not disagree with her bitter indictment of the modern world, he simply cannot think of anything to say. She attacks him and denounces what she considers his new solution to life's problems:

> Your discovery, as best as I can determine, is that there is an alternative which no one has hit upon. It is that one finding oneself in one of life's critical situations need not after all respond in one of the traditional ways. No. One may simply default. Pass. Do as one pleases, shrug, turn on one's heel and leave. Exit.

In all this he is a straight outsider, a man alienated from his neighbours, and unable to subscribe to their values, allegiances and verdicts. His solution however—an extreme one, indeed—is to try and become as ordinary as possible, to carve a reliable niche for himself in normality and routine. He has given up ambition, abandoned the "old longings," taken a suburban apartment, addicted himself to television and filled his wallet with "identity cards, library cards, credit cards." "It is a pleasure to carry out the duties of a citizen and to receive in return a receipt or a neat styrene card with one's name on it certifying, so to speak, one's right to exist." He gives himself up wholly to his business, making money and dating his secretaries. But his motives have nothing in common with Seymour [Glass's] desire to bless and embrace what he secretly despises. Binx Bolling's aim is to keep the nightmare of metaphysical lostness and unreality at bay. The worst threat—and travelling from place to place makes the threat acute—is that one day he may wake up and "find himself No one and Nowhere." This is why, unlike most American heroes, he hates to travel. A visit to Chicago disturbs him greatly, leading him to assert:

> Every place of arrival should have a booth set up and manned by an ordinary person whose task it is to greet strangers and give them a little trophy of local spacetime stuff—tell them of his difficulties in high school and put a pinch of soil in their pockets—in order to insure that the stranger shall not become an Anyone.

Like Zooey [Glass] he needs ballast: but not to prevent his premature ascension to heaven, only to stave off the complete dissolution of his identity. It is this need which makes him mark his cinema seat with his thumbnail. It is a way of reminding himself that he was Some where at Some time, and not Any where in Any time.

It is for this reason that he is a moviegoer, that he remembers incidents from films more vividly than he can recall incidents from his own life. It is not that films give romance where romance is lacking, nor that they offer the escape of a dream world. Rather they render fixed and inevitable what in life seems to him to be fluid and contingent. He is fascinated by the "peculiar reality" of movie stars, and movies themselves bestow images of reality on a world which seems in danger of losing any conviction as to its very existence. In particular if you see your own world in a film, then your world is "certified." He explains:

> Nowadays when a person lives somewhere, in a neighborhood, the place is not certified for him. More than likely he will live there sadly and the emptiness which is inside of him will expand until it evacuates the entire neighborhood. But if he sees a movie which shows his very neighborhood, it becomes possible for him

to live, for a time at least, as a person who is Somewhere and not Anywhere.

That it requires the movies to give man this certification of the reality of his own world merely indicates what deserts of unreality the modern alienated wonderer finds himself stumbling through.

But there is one big difference between the American Moviegoer and the French Outsider. For there recurs to Binx Bolling "the possibility of a search." Now, it is hard to think of many major American novels which do not in some way incorporate in them the notion of a search, a quest, a more than physical journey—whether one thinks of Captain Ahab or Augie March, Huck Finn or Albert Strether or Jay Gatsby. For Binx Bolling the search is finally for a true wonder, a maintained curiosity, an inviolable sense of reality. Of course the "search" has nothing to do with a spell of worldwide sight-seeing (he loathes the idea of a *Wanderjahr* very much as Zooey detests "any kind of so-called creative type who gets on any kind of a ship"). The search is into the "here and now," not away from it. He first had the idea of a search when he came to his senses after being wounded in the war. "Six inches from my nose a dung beetle was scratching around under the leaves. As I watched, there awoke in me an immense curiosity. I was onto something. I vowed that if I ever got out of this fix, I would pursue the search. Naturally, as soon as I recovered and got home, I forgot all about it." The idea recurs to him one morning when he suddenly sees the odds and ends on his dressing table as though for the first time. He wonders at them, insignificant scraps though they are. "What was unfamiliar about them was that I could see them. They might have belonged to someone else." This is to cease to take reality for granted, to be restored to a sense of the miraculousness as well as the gratuitousness of the stuff around us. He then defines the search in the following way:

> The search is what anyone would undertake if he were not sunk in the everydayness of his own life. This morning, for example, I felt as if I had come to myself on a strange island. And what does such a castaway do? Why, he pokes around his neighborhood and he doesn't miss a trick.
>
> To become aware of the possibility of the search is to be onto something. Not to be onto something is to be in despair.

The terms are vague but the main point is clear. To be sunk in everydayness, to be bored, blasé, or complacently unaware of mystery, to have lost the sense of wonder—is to be dead. More interesting for our purpose is the narrator's description of the two different kinds of search he has conducted. There was the vertical search: "During those years I stood outside the universe and sought to understand it. . . . The only difficulty was that though the universe had been disposed of, I myself was left over." This search had been concerned with discovering the governing laws of life from books like *The Expanding Universe* and *The Chemistry of Life*. These laws could not, however, explain the mystery of his own presence. So he moved to the horizontal search. "As a consequence, what takes place in my room is less important. What is important is what I shall find when I leave my room and wander in the neighborhood. Before, I wandered as a diversion. Now I wander seriously and sit and read as a diversion." The two terms neatly echo the conflict of inclination we noted in so many American writers, a desire to pierce the sky wrestling with an instinct to align themselves with the ground. Binx Bolling's decision to move to the horizontal search is of a piece with Thoreau's resolution to turn away from the Universal Law and seek for truth in particular instances. With the vertical search you approach that Universal Law: "you understand more and more specimens by fewer and fewer formulae. . . . Of course you are always after the big one, the new key, the secret leverage point, and that is the best of it." Except that the perceiving enraptured individual gets left out. Whereas with the horizontal search, as Kate interprets it, "if you sit back here and take a little carcass out of the garbage can, a specimen which has been used and discarded, there remains something left over, a clue." The scrap from the garbage can—the pebble by your foot: it is yet another expression of the recurring American resolution to start with the nearest and next, the potluck of the day, the small proximate particular.

The habit of wonder is, for Binx Bolling, superior to all scientific and intellectual modes of inquiry: and here we see a typical American suspicion or prejudice discharging itself. Thus he once tried to do scientific research to please his aunt; but his interest faded and "I became extraordinarily affected by the summer afternoons in the laboratory." His co-worker became a dedicated and successful scientist.

> Yet I do not envy him. . . . For he is no more aware of the mystery which surrounds him than a fish is aware of the water it swims in. He could do research for a thousand years and never have an inkling of it. By the middle of August I could not see what difference it made whether the pigs got kidney stones or not (they didn't incidentally), compared to the mystery of those summer afternoons.

And later, when his aunt insists on praising his "analytical mind" he takes pains to inform us that "I have never analyzed anything." Only wondered at everything. Even an old dilapidated cinema fills him with "a secret sense of wonder about the enduring, about all the nights, the rainy summer nights at twelve and one and two o'clock when the seats endured alone in the empty theater. The enduring is something which must be accounted for. One cannot simply shrug it off." This refusal to shrug off the mystery of life and the concomitant suspicion of all inquiry without wonder, is, of course, very sympathetic. It is just worth noting, however, that once the hero (and this applies now to many American books) has opted for this stance of reverent wonder to the exclusion of all other forms of response, there is very little he can do except reiterate his sense of wonder. This can lead to the repetitious and ultimately boring, even unconvincing enthusiasm of a Jack Kerouac. It can lead, as we have seen throughout the book, to endless formal problems— what shall the artist do with what he wonders at apart from list it? To set up "wonder" as the *only* adequate response to reality is impoverishing, and to assert that it alone can approach the rare mystery of life is untrue. Binx Bolling can no more "account" for the endurance of an old cinema than a scientist can account for the miraculous fact that the matter he explains exists at all. But there can surely be forms of science not divorced from wonder just as there can be intellectual activity not devoid of reverence: to set up such simplifying antinomies seems to me an unfortunate late-romantic sentimentality. In terms of the book we nevertheless feel the rightness of Binx Bolling's preferences and his sense of wonder is balanced by his intelligence, his irony, and his well-regulated dislike for the moribund niceness of the society which surrounds him.

The novel solution of this alienated wonderer is to hide himself deep inside ordinary society, for there he can wander incognito, secretly raging against "the great shithouse of scientific humanism," with his "nose for merde" and his eye for wonder as his two most precious assets. One could say that, in a different way, Salinger also employs those highly developed organs. And so does Huck Finn, and Nick Adams, and the young narrator of Sherwood Anderson's "I want to know why"—the list extends itself. If we call the two responses wonder and horror we can draw in many of Henry James's protagonists: substitute "a suspicion of society" for horror, and Emerson, Thoreau and Whitman appear without incongruity. What all these writers stress in their various ways is the radical importance of a true way of seeing; the generous, open, even naive, undulled and reverent eye—as opposed to the self-interested squinting and peering of the greedy utilitarian social eye, and the cold myopia of the scientific, analytic eye. Their ideal is an eye of passive wonder. "Saints Behold" announced the Transcendentalists: "perpetual observation, perpetual acquiescence" was Emerson's favourite stance: "You might say of a philosopher that he was in this world as a spectator" wrote Thoreau: Whitman wanted to be "in and out of the game, watching and wondering at it": "observe perpetually" advised James. Sherwood Anderson simply "wanted to spend my life walking about and looking at things": the Moviegoer likes to "listen to people, see how they stick themselves into the world": "Judgment is second to wonder" for Saul Bellow's first narrator: "WATCH" was Seymour's favourite word in the Bible.

Emerson almost wrote a creed for all the writers we have discussed when he stressed the prime importance, for the artist, of "revelation, always a miracle, which no frequency of occurrence or incessant study can ever familiarize, but which must always leave the inquirer stupid with wonder." But as the wonderer has become more and more alienated, the things miraculously revealed to him are not always such as will leave him "stupid with wonder": sometimes he is stupefied with nausea, sometimes paralysed with horror. These reactions may be called "first step" reactions; and perhaps we may just hazard the generalization that, finding themselves the new inhabitants of a new world (a world which had not been properly looked at before), American writers had first of all to see "like children" before they could go on to see like men. The strange fact is that very few of them managed to make that development. Scott Fitzgerald's remark that the lives of American writers have no second acts could perhaps be adapted to read—American writers find it extremely difficult to take second steps. From the start European models offered them almost no help with their basic problem—how to absorb and arrange American experience. The "first step" of somehow assimilating the clamorous undifferentiated stuff around them required tremendous energy and effort and often seems to have exhausted American writers. If there is a sort of habit of itemizing discernible in Whitman and other writers then that is because itemization is at least the beginning of differentiation; and without differentiation art is impossible and man is the mere victim of impressions which yield no meanings, of things which express no values. But this primal act of differentiation and assimilation will not, of itself, produce art. For that there is required some sense of ordered form. And it is noticeable that American writers have found it unusually difficult to discover helpful modes of organization, fruitful forms which will guide without enslaving, encircling devices which will aid in the necessary ordering of intensities.

It may seem rather arid and conservative to insist on the value and necessity of form, almost abstractly considered; but I should stress that I am far from insisting on the superior value of any one particular sort of form. Rather, by "form" I mean some prior notion of shaping intent, some initial focus which directs vision without determining results. I mean that which produces architecture and not mere aggregates. Since the very protoplasmic stuff of life is not aimless but on the contrary exhibits a formative capacity, a regulatory purposive activity, an indefatigable tendency towards complex but stable organization, it is perhaps inevitable that art must have at least as much organization if it is to live. If we do uphold organic theories of art then it should be to insist that a work of art exhibits, not as much way-wardness as nature's processes, but as much self-maintaining and coordi-nated structure as nature's products. But a work of art is more than a work of nature. Nature organizes herself to survive; art is organized to discover and display meanings and values. And without some sense of form that indispensable work of discovery can scarcely begin. The formed work per-petuates values and meanings: the unformed work records sensations and accidents.

Nearly all American writers have found it difficult to move beyond the first step, to find satisfactory forms. This phenomenon poses a problem which is obviously beyond the scope of this [essay]. But we are in a position to offer a few tentative partial explanations. The passive wonder which con-stitutes the preferred mode of vision of so many of the writers we have discussed is a valid strategy of assimilation, but of itself it can neither gen-erate nor discover form. It can isolate and vivify details and facts; but if, as Emerson advised, you ask the fact for the form, the fact has a habit of not answering. As so much American writing demonstrates. For although pas-sivity may promote a state of rich appreciation, it can never produce the means of embodying and projecting that appreciation: passivity can never effect that necessary transformation of private impressions into communi-cated values. Art is inherently active: passive creation is a contradiction in terms. Art is indebted to the natural given world for its materials: but it adds to nature new arrangings which reveal significances. It forcefully separates things from chaos and flux and sets them in new contexts, new configura-tions which radiate and preserve values and insights. And to achieve this a positive act of inquiry and penetration is required. Sheer awareness must give way to something more active if it is to develop a style. This leads us to our second clue.

Many American writers have shown a persistent antipathy to "analysis." (Of course from one point of view this can be subsumed under the general romantic nineteenth-century distaste for "analysis": but there is something specially, and significantly, virulent and programmatic, even fearful, in the

American attitude.) In American writing the word is nearly always used pejoratively, and a deep-rooted hostility to the analysing faculties is as obvious in Salinger's and Percy's novels as it is in Emerson and Thoreau. (A typical gesture of repugnance can be found in a letter from Mark Twain to Howells written in 1885 where he complains that George Eliot "analyzes the guts" out of "motives and feelings.") When Baudelaire affirmed that "genius is nothing more or less than *childhood recovered* at will "he was expressing an appreciation of the rapture of infantile habits of perception and response which many American writers have shared. But Baudelaire went on to add these significant words: "a childhood now equipped for self-expression with manhood's capacities and *a power of analysis which enables it to order the mass of raw material which it has involuntarily accumulated.*" (My italics—the passage can be found in his essay "The Painter of Modern Life.") Here, as I suggested at the outset, is a major difference between European and American literature since the romantic movement. In American writing one hears much about "recovered childhood" but very little about the ordering "power of analysis" which Baudelaire deemed indispensable to artistic creation: the result is, I maintain, that we often meet with a great deal of "involuntary accumulation." Mind and intellect are too often the villains in American literature. Yet, as Thomas Mann said, "mind is life's self-criticism": it is also an important agent of life's self-evaluation. It is ultimately perverse and crippling to deny it an important part in the creation of works of art. Without some sort of analysis there can be no second steps, no fully realized form. It is the necessary prelude to a new synthesis. Of course these observations by no means exhaust the problem. Hawthorne and Melville were both active inquirers and courageous analysts, and yet they too had difficulty in finding enabling forms. In Hawthorne's case it would seem that there was so much guilt attached to analysis that his appalled conscience unsettled and unnerved his probing mind until the stable form of *The Scarlet Letter* finally gives way to the unbalanced confusion of *The Marble Faun*. Melville also seems to have experienced some of this guilt. *Moby Dick* does after all explore the fatal blasphemy of a Faustian man—though, of course, it took a Faustian man to write it. This great book indeed does have a profound inner organization which easily contains any surface shifts and inconsistencies: the relentless focus and indelible imprint of a great mind and imagination at full stretch are everywhere in evidence. Yet *Pierre* reveals that same mind perturbed and harassed to a point where it can no longer organize its materials: things get out of proportion, perspective fails, and the form all but tears itself to pieces. *Billy Budd* and a few of the short stories display a compressed unremitting relevance which indicates Melville's intermittent mastery of form: but the long years of silence and the unprofitable experiments with verse lead one to suspect that a prolonged inability to find satisfactory forms had a stifling effect on the greatest of all American imaginations. Henry James could never have written anything as great as *Moby Dick,* but his endless preoccupation with problems of form and his serene employment of the intelligence did enable him to produce consistently and continuously. He took step after step and made discovery after discovery. Scott Fitzgerald was perhaps the only successor to James who did justice to the attitude of wonder and also moved towards an increasingly profound analysis of it—its shortcomings and frailties, its poetry and its fate. He responded to "the dream," but turned an increasingly acute eye to the "foul dust" that "floated in the wake." Into the figure of Gatsby he put much of what he admired in America: a "heightened sensitivity to the promise of life . . . an extraordinary gift for hope, a romantic readiness." There is something in Gatsby's generous, ideal aspirations which transcends their sordid base and survives their squalid destiny. His hopes are visionary, even though his end is coldly actual. "Out of the corner of his eye Gatsby saw that the blocks of the sidewalk really formed a ladder and mounted to a secret place above the trees—he could climb to it, if he climbed alone, and once there he could suck the pap of life, gulp down the incomparable milk of wonder." Fitzgerald is remarkable because he never blinks the gaudiness and sentimentality, indeed the almost majestic vulgarity of Gatsby's imagination, yet he can catch what is truly lyrical and valuable and rare in the spirit behind it. He never fell into cynical disillusion even though he went on to show how inwardly fallible and outwardly foredoomed the wondering idealist was. Like those Dutch sailors he thought that America brought man "face to face for the last time in history with something commensurate to his capacity for wonder" and he celebrated that capacity at the same time as he traced it to its doom. His early work is over-ebullient, too romantic, vulnerable: but his later work shows a sober, compassionate analytic power which points, not to the indignity of the "crack-up," but to a growing artistic maturity. It does seem as though Fitzgerald's determination to explore the *limits* of wonder, to celebrate the poetry of its willingness *and* draw the perspectives of its fate, helped him towards an increasingly firm formal control of his material.

Of course none of the works we have examined is totally without form and where we think we can detect faltering or failure we may be in the presence of some exciting and enriching experiment, some challengingly new form. But often this form has been one which does not countenance further explorations and facilitate further discoveries. Few of the writers we mentioned found forms which would help to stimulate a deepening complexity of response. How many great American writers have really triumphed only in one book!

Despite the many difficulties American writers have had to face, American literature is already immensely rich and fertile. However, one might fairly make a certain limiting judgment on its very real wealth by suggesting that it has often shown an inability to move beyond one particular syndrome of responses—wonder keeling over into horror, delight switching to disillusion, revulsion locked with awe. It has shown itself, perhaps, too suspicious of the analytical intellect, too disinclined to develop a complex reaction to society, too much given to extreme reactions, too hungry for metaphysics. In style it has, at times, been too sedulous in its indiscriminate attention to details, or too apt to avoid complexity by leaping to the refuge of vague generalizations. And yet all these shortcomings are but the extremes of its virtues: its great personal integrity, its noble refusal of complacency and compromise, its compassion and generosity and humor, its energy, its unremitting craving for reality and its reverent love for the world. It was with no idle phrase that Scott Fitzgerald described America as "a willingness of the heart." At their best the writers we have discussed do what all artists should do—replenish and revivify our vision of the world. They approach with awe areas of existence which most men are prepared to exploit or ignore; they give the world back into our reinvigorated keeping, they enhance reality for us. An indispensable wonder comes through.

FREDERICK C. CREWS

The Hero as "Case": The Last Gentleman

The American novelist who would appear up-to-date must go through certain familiar motions. He must assure us at once that he isn't recounting a story but establishing a style, an adequate manner of coping with the zany modern world. He must replace characterization with caricature, and stamp "Artifact" on every page lest we mistake him for, say, Sinclair Lewis. He must be horrible and cool, morbid and funny, sex-ridden and bored with sex. And he must never look inward, for it is understood that the personal psyche has been thoroughly explored and found uninteresting. With luck the talented writer who follows these rules will puzzle Orville Prescott with his obscurity, please Leslie Fiedler with his courageous negativism, and begin to nudge the older-style bestsellers off the list.

If Walker Percy disdains this path to success, it is not because he is slower-witted than the pop novelists. He too thinks that America is weird, sex largely comic, and the dead just plain dead. But there is a difference: these ideas *matter* to him and to his characters, and they must be painfully learned rather than decoratively embodied in grotesqueries of plotting. Thus, though Percy's second novel does aim at making a broad statement about the modern condition and has its moments of heavyhanded symbolism, it does no great violence to the conventions of realistic fiction. Like most good novels before the present era, it assumes that characters have souls to be won or lost, or at any rate to be lost in better or worse ways.

From *Commentary* 42, no. 3 (September 1966). © 1966 by The American Jewish Committee. Originally entitled "The Hero as 'Case.'"

Percy's uniqueness is genuine but hard to pin down. The thematic trappings of *The Last Gentleman* are so familiar—Civil War nostalgia, religious zeal, racial tension, the vulgar New South and the anonymous North—that it might be mistakenly regarded as belonging to the school of lapsed-Baptist regionalism. In fact, Percy is a remarkably fastidious writer who would never permit himself a cliché of any sort. His manner as a storyteller is that of his hero: "the amiable and slightly ironic air which Southerners find natural away from home." And the story he has to tell is only incidentally regional; its three locales of New York, Alabama, and New Mexico are meant almost as the steps of a philosophical proof. Perhaps this abstraction is Percy's keynote. Brilliant though he is in satirizing what lies before him, his attention is fixed on the absoluteness of death and the impossibility of genuine intimacy. The proof to which he submits his hero is that these ultimate facts can be temporarily mitigated only if one accepts a limited role and pretends to be immersed in it. When the hero finally heads back toward his native Alabama to sell Chevrolets, it is not at all because he has discovered that he belongs there, but because he has seen that the alternative is suicide.

Percy's demonstration requires that all his major characters illustrate the same underlying predicament. All are Southerners maladapted to the hustling, secular world of urban America. The most confused and malleable of them is naturally the hero, Will Barrett. He does excellently on aptitude tests but can't think what to do between tests, and sometimes he quite literally forgets who he is. Suffering alternately from *déjà vus* and amnesia, haunted by the Civil War and by the suicide of his antiracist father, unable to stomach his ordained role as a Princeton man, waiting for a sign that will narrow the seemingly infinite possibilities of his life, he attaches himself to the Vaught family in New York, routinely falls in love with the younger daughter, follows them all to Alabama, and watches the younger brother die of an incurable disease in Santa Fe. Each character he meets and each station of his passive pilgrimage bring him closer to the wry but serviceable disillusion he possesses at the end.

The most important of Barrett's teachers, the one who frames Percy's dilemma most articulately, is Sutter Vaught, a gifted physician who is slowly destroying himself because (so he believes) scientific theory has made all his human relations "transcendent." He epitomizes the refined Southerner who can neither accept the present nor forget the past; he is obsessed in particular with the breakdown of courtship, and he takes private revenge on the emancipated ladies of America by seducing them perfunctorily. Such forays into the "immanence" of the flesh only feed his cynicism. His sister, Val, equally disoriented by consumer democracy, has taken refuge in Catholic sacramentalism and missionary work; she is waiting irrelevantly for an apocalypse that is not forthcoming. Sister Kitty, Barrett's fiancée, would like to be a coy belle, and Barrett himself approves of this stereotype; but she is even more anxious to prove her sexual capacity. As Sutter writes in his notebook, "Now one begins with genital overtures instead of a handshake, then waits to see what will turn up (e.g., we might become friends later)." And another brother, Jamie Vaught, is mentally sound but drifting toward an ugly death that will show Barrett conclusively that he had better cease trusting in destiny. When he finally decides to marry the conformist Kitty and join the Chevrolet agency of her suffocatingly beneficent father, it is clear that he has Percy's endorsement. If life is mysterious, lonely, and terrible, the novel seems to say, the thing to do is to find a convenient way of blotting out the truth.

The power of *The Last Gentleman* doesn't depend on the validity of this disappointing syllogism. In most respects the book is solid and admirable, full of brilliant observation and subtle thought. Though Percy has a certain difficulty maneuvering his characters from one suitably meaningful backdrop to another, the general development is patient and coherent. And the closing episode of Jamie's death, with its gruesome hassle over baptism and its wrenching combination of sympathy and clinical detail, is stronger than anything in Percy's notable first novel, *The Moviegoer.*

Yet the total effect is somehow pale. Because it is finally a literal story, *The Last Gentleman* depends heavily on the felt intensity of Will Barrett's plight, and Barrett never comes across very emphatically. Though he feels constantly dissatisfied, suffers sudden lapses, and allows himself to be molded by every chance occurrence, he remains oddly insulated from his conflicts. Some of his emotional substance, as with Hawthorne's Robin Molineux or James Purdy's Malcolm, has been drained off into the symbolic vicissitudes he undergoes, so that we can puzzle out his "case" in a detached way by interpreting his various mishaps; but such an understanding is no substitute for the existential anguish Percy would like us to feel.

Indeed, I am not sure that Percy would approve of our regarding Will Barrett as a "case" at all. His explicit psychological remarks as a narrator are designedly superficial; he really prefers to see Barrett as Modern Man, or at any rate to play off his apparent symptoms against the more serious unhealthiness of the times. Barrett's amnesia, which disappears as soon as he has decided to begin selling Chevvies, is meant as nothing more than a device to underline his identity crisis, and his *déjà vus* are likewise devices for bringing the past thematically to bear upon that crisis. His New York psychoanalyst learns virtually nothing about his mind in five years of expensive banter, and Percy hints that after all there is nothing worth learning.

Yet the "case" is nonetheless there to be discerned. Barrett is an orphan in search of a surrogate family, and his attitudes are in some respects those of an adolescent scandalized by sex. He is an eavesdropper by temperament; even when he falls in love it is while spying with his telescope in Central Park. His habitual indecision is related to this streak of voyeurism: "he had to know everything before he could do anything." He is disgusted by the ease with which he has seduced Kitty, yet, as he confesses to Sutter, he has yearned for "the coarsest possible relations" with women generally. And Sutter, whom he is excessively anxious to obey, perceives why Barrett is so sheepish with him: "You either want me to tell you to fornicate or not to fornicate, but for the life of me I can't tell which it is." These and many other details fit into a classic Oedipal pattern, whether or not Percy intends them to.

There should be nothing either surprising or damaging in the possibility that a novelist has not fully calculated the inner consistency of his hero's behavior; so far as I can tell, this is the rule with interesting fiction. A difficulty arises only if the author, taking a superficial view of his handiwork, mistakes the hero for an Everyman whose problems are the exigencies of universal reality. Percy does not seem aware that the moral extremes to which Barrett and Sutter are drawn—lewdness versus saintliness, suicide versus salesmanship—are appropriate only to a particular adolescent crisis. Dostoevsky, it may be said, had the same predilection for seeing the decisions of his driven heroes as metaphysical imperatives; but in Dostoevsky the suffering that precedes those decisions is a primary reality that does not have to be established by symbolism or theory. If *The Last Gentleman,* despite its substantial virtues, finally fails to make a deep impression, the reason may be that Percy does not care either to inspect Will Barrett's conflicts at close range or to understand them much more clearly than Barrett does himself.

MARTIN LUSCHEI

The Ruins of Consensus:
Love in the Ruins

THE TRIAL OF TOM MORE

We return not to the thrilling days of yesteryear, but to a seemingly casual event three days earlier: "Someone took a shot at me at the breakfast table." This shot, quickly followed by two more, opens the novel as the first incident taking place in its present time. The three shots launch the action and also place us subliminally, touching the collective nerve of a nation traumatized by three shots in Dallas: the novel speaks not to an Auto Age, as Tom often refers to our own era, but to that Gothic era of assassinations identified with the name Kennedy. And Tom's response belongs equally to the same period: "As I was considering this at the top of my head, something at the heart of me knew better and I found myself diving for the corner even as I ruminated." He saves himself by "a reflex learned with the First Air Cav in the fifteen year war in Ecuador"—the conditioned response of an American of the 1960s.

The public nature of such conditioning is appropriate here, for now begins the public phase of Tom's ordeal. A later and more private one is to follow, but the first campaign of his war on two fronts takes place under the lights, so to speak, in the long middle sequence of the novel culminating in the comic shoot-out between Tom and Buddy Brown. Later the focus will turn inward; here it is on *them,* as the consensus anthropology is tested in the comic fires of The Pit.

From *The Sovereign Wayfarer: Walker Percy's Diagnosis of the Malaise.* © 1972 by Louisiana State University Press. Originally entitled "The Ruins of Consensus."

As the contest opens the odds seem overwhelmingly against our shaky eccentric hero. On his forty-fifth birthday Tom lies on the floor of his enclosed patio, out of the line of fire, thinking of Doris, his lost wife. He is the perfect model of Kierkegaard's man whose house is without a beloved. Tom's prospects are not enhanced by what follows. At the moment of the first shot he is sipping Tang, drinking it warm because nothing works any more, not even his refrigerator. The USA went down the drain not because of polarization or pornography, he says; "what finally tore it was that things stopped working and nobody wanted to be a repairman." He lies there looking up at Doris's books, swollen by rains to "fat wads of pulp": *Siddhartha, Atlas Shrugged, ESP and the New Spirituality*. Poor Doris had fallen victim to a weakness common to a certain type of Episcopal girl "just past youth"; she was ruined by "spiritual books" and "Gnostic pride."

The past comes into the story now as Tom lies ruminating about the last time he made love to her, here in the "enclosed patio," shortly before her departure with Alistair Fuchs-Forbes and his chum. "Here was where I had set a record: that of all cuckolds in history, I am the first American to be cuckolded by *two* English fruits." The scene recalled is good comic Percy. Tom presses what she insists upon calling his "conjugal rights" while Doris mouths one cliché after another from the new spirituality: "I'm going in search of myself"; "love should be a joyous encounter"; "spiritual growth is the law of life." She is en route to "making herself whole" at Alistair's handicraft retreat in Cozumel, the "last hope of the Western world," where "transcendental religion could rescue Western materialism." "We're so dead, Tom," she explains. Alistair is a "very tragic person. But he's a searcher like me, a pilgrim." The notions of people as dead and man as searcher or pilgrim are very nearly Percy's own. He satirizes her understanding of them, I think, because the worst enemy of truth often is not its opposite, error, but its next of kin, the cliché that encases and smothers it. "Pilgrim my ass," Tom says.

A serious note enters with mention of Samantha's death. Percy does not linger on it, merely introduces it; her death becomes important later, in the private phase of Tom's ordeal. Some eight years earlier Samantha had died a horrible death. Tom thinks Doris left because she never forgave him or God for it: "'That's a loving God you have there,' she told me toward the end, when the neuroblastoma had pushed one eye out and around the nose-bridge so that Samantha looked like a two-eyed Picasso profile." He and Doris "chose not to forgive each other," he says later, and Alistair "happened to come along at the right time. Lacking forgiveness, Tom took to drink and Doris to the new spirituality, two familiar responses to great personal loss.

Doris died and Tom's life moved into ever deepening shadows. So much for the remote past, which is prologue to his present state.

We get a glimpse of the more recent past through Dusty Rhoades, who gives Tom a lift to the Country Club in his bubble-top Toyota. Tom has evaded the sniper, at least for now. Dusty Rhoades is a fitting name for the conservative proctologist from Texas who has bought a plantation house called Tara and seeks to revive that faded apparition. Last Christmas Eve, Dusty had found his beautiful daughter, Lola, in Tom's arms in the deep grassy bunker of the eighteenth hole, a bit of "misbehavior in Paradise" for which he has not forgiven Tom. While they roll along listening to "Hills of Home," the Tara theme and Dusty's favorite tune, Dusty gives Tom to understand that the only honorable course open to him is to marry Lola and move into Tara: "You going to do right by Lola, or Doctor, I'm going to have your ass. Is that clear?"

In the meantime, as they clear Security at the sentry box and enter the "inner circle of Paradise," Tom has brought out his lapsometer and taken a reading on Dusty. He shows almost no coeliac anxiety, this "ex-fullback and hardworking surgeon, a man at home with himself and too busy to worry" about his pineal selfhood; "he may fear one thing or another but he's not afraid of no-thing, which is the worst of fears." But his love-sex ratio is reversed: "the reading from Brodmann Area 24, the locus of 'higher' or interpersonal relations, is a tiny 0.5 mmv while the hypothalamus, seat of organic sexual activity, registers a whacking stud-level 7.9 mmv," the wave of a "powerful, frequently satisfied, but indiscriminate sexual appetite." Dusty sees through Tom's evasions ("What you're saying is I'm messing around with my nurses") and demands to know if the lapsometer is "nonpartisan": "Does it also measure alcoholism, treachery, laziness, and whitetrash morals?" An astute Knothead, fully polarized, as befits the proprietor of Tara in the new Southern Paradise, Dusty grasps the political implications of the lapsometer instantly. Here is the exemplar of bestialism.

The empty pro shop reminds Tom of the affair with Lola, whom he had kissed there. "Women are mythical creatures," he remarks, thinking of the beautiful six-foot Lola with her gin fizz in hand. The memory prompts one of those ecstatic cries that recur as a motif throughout the novel: "Women! Music! Love! Life! Joy! Gin fizzes!" The theme is Percy's ode to joy, related to Kierkegaard's realm of the musical erotic; and like the retort to the waiting buzzards noted earlier it affirms life in the face of death, woe, and plain befuddlement. Tom, having only that day perfected his lapsometer and finished his article, is suffering from "simultaneous depression and exaltation."

Why? Lola wants to know. "Well, I've won, you see. Won the big one. But it's Christmas Eve and I'm alone. My family is dead. There's nobody to tell." So he tells Lola, of course. "Her company stabilizes me. Abstracted still, my orbit becomes lower." Note what happens. Tom remains abstracted—semi-angelized, we might say—but his orbit swings nearer the human—the condition of man as man. "Bending close to her, close to the upper reaches of her breast, is like skimming in silence, power off, over the snowy slopes of Kilimanjaro."

Lola, who is united with herself in her love of music, "goes dreaming through the world safe and sure as Schubert's trout." A few "snapshots" of her with Tom's "Brownie," the lapsometer, reveal zero anxiety but an interpersonal wave "both powerful and truncated, lopped off at the peak like Popocatepetl." She has "a heart full of love and no one to give it to." It is inevitable that the muddled psychiatrist is soon "singing like a cello" between the knees of the lovely cellist. There seems to be no Puritanical note here, just as there is none in the musical-erotic realm described by Kierkegaard, for which the cello is such an apt metaphor. The Percyan touch comes immediately thereafter when Tom becomes engorged with lymph and Lola saves his life at the cost of her reputation. "She could have gone, left me to die in the bunker, swell up and die and be found stiff as a poker in the foggy dew." But she fetched help, and Dusty, who found Tom without breath and "in some disarray," shot him full of epinephrine and brought him out of it. As his Christmas Eve then resumed its original plan, Tom watched Perry Como, now "seventy years young and snowy-thatched but hale as old Saint Nick himself," sitting on his stool singing "Silent Night" on the stereo-V.

Evidently it was on Christmas morning, after listening to Perry Como, that Tom attempted suicide. Tom himself is not quite sure about it, but certainly watching Perry Como, "face orange, lips violet," do his youth act—that despairing travesty on a travesty of the Christmas spirit—would unsettle a man. Having been "assaulted at night by longings, succubi, and the hideous shellfire of Verdun," he awoke with his wrists cut and bleeding. "Seeing the blood, I came to myself, saw myself as itself and the world for what it is, and began to love life." Like any castaway of Percy's he took inventory: "After all, why not live? Bad as things are still when all is said and done, one can sit on a doorstep in the winter sunlight and watch sparrows kick leaves." Brought out of orbit by Lola only to be swamped in the despair of Como's Christmas, Tom comes to himself through ordeal and is rescued by the small concrete favors of life, winter sunlight and sparrows kicking leaves.

His friend Max Gottlieb sutures his arteries without much ado. Tom recovers sufficiently to invite Ellen Oglethorpe, the nurse, to his bed, somewhat after the fashion of Frederic Henry. But she declines, and his lust yielding to sorrow, he prays, "arms stretched out like a Mexican" and tears streaming down his face: "Dear God, I can see it now, why can't I see it at other times, that it is you I love in the beauty of the world and in all the lovely girls and dear good friends, and it is pilgrims we are, wayfarers on a journey, and not pigs, nor angels. Why can I not be merry and loving like my ancestor, a gentle pure-hearted knight for our Lady and blessed Lord and Savior? Pray for me, Sir Thomas More." Percy follows deprecatingly with an "etcetera etcetera," but this passage without a trace of irony is a key to Tom's condition. He exists in a state of sin, which for Kierkegaard is the opposite not of virtue but of faith. Sin for Kierkegaard "does not consist in the fact that man has not understood what is right, but in the fact that he will not understand it, and in the fact that he will not do it." Tom More is not Will Barrett; in his case "there is this little tiny transition from having understood to doing." The good "must be done at once," Kierkegaard says, but the "strength of the lower nature consists in dragging a thing out." The will has no objection, and "when the intelligence has become duly darkened" the two of them can "understand one another better" because the intelligence has surrendered to the will. The everydayness duly darkening Tom's awareness is this understanding between his intelligence and his will. Ordeal rends it momentarily, and he recognizes himself to be the wayfarer he scorns in the fraudulent platitudes of Doris. It remains to be seen whether his condition will benefit by this fleeting insight.

The upshot of his suicide attempt was that he committed himself to the federal hospital, from which he went AWOL the following May, a couple of months before the novel's action begins. At present he is on his way back to the hospital to see Max.

Moving by stealth toward his objective, trying to outwit the sniper, Tom stumbles upon a conspiracy in the pagoda shelter on an island in the golf course. A three-man contingent of blacks is conversing beyond a partition while the Christian Kaydettes, a ridiculous marching group of baton twirlers, rehearse on the parade ground not far off. The plan of the blacks is to capture the Kaydettes on the Fourth of July and somehow to conscript the Ph.D.'s at Fedville as teachers for black children at the Honey Island school. A contrast emerges between Victor Charles, a local man who knows the whites and wants no one hurt, and Uru, a militant from the North untroubled by such misgivings. To the presumably sophisticated Uru, Victor is a hopeless Uncle Tom. Uru is an uprooted figure who belongs nowhere, with "a voice without antecedents, black yes, Midwestern perhaps, but mainly stereo-V, an announcer's voice, a Detroit disc jockey's voice." The three of them have shot a deer to feed the starving black children whose fathers have been put out of work as a result of Charley Parker's tinkering. "Well," says Willard Amadie, Tom's former caddy, "they going to eat today."

Tom moves on to the hospital and his old ward where his "old friends and fellow madmen" live: "They gaze at me, knowing me and knowing me not. I am like a dream they have dreamed before. A man standing at the window twitters his fingers, sending out radar beams to the vague, gauzy world, and cocks his ear, listening for returning blips. *Who are you out there?*" This is where he spent the best months of his life. "Here in the day room and in the ward we patients came to understand each other as only fellow prisoners and exiles can." The theme is familiar Percy: sanity in such times is not man's everyday condition, which is apt to be a pernicious despair, but a state of awareness to which one most likely comes through ordeal, perhaps through "madness" itself. True sanity resides in Being rather than in non-Being. The world outside the hospital, when Tom leaves the ward and goes AWOL, is almost too much, and Percy renders the moment phenomenologically in one sentence, as he often does in this novel: "Wham! there it was, the world, solid as a rock, dense as a doorknob."

Tom's return to the ward produces a confrontation in which things are not at all what they seem. We see the sanity of "madness" and the insanity of "science" in the form of behaviorism as Percy's phenomenological treatment begins to yield dividends. The scene is crucial to his purpose because if the perspective of the novel is to be fully realized the reader must enter into it at this point.

Tom has a practical objective in coming to see Max: he wants Max to support his effort to secure funds for a crash program by which to develop his lapsometer and thus ward off disaster—a "mad" ambition, surely, though the reader can see the sanity of it. "Let's talk about this sense of impending disaster," Max says, therapist fashion, in the language by which demons are banished and a firm grip kept on the familiar world. He speaks common sense edified by science. But Tom detects "an oddity": "Max the unbeliever, a lapsed Jew, believes in the orderliness of creation, acts on it with energy and charity. I the believer, having swallowed the whole Thing, God Jews Christ Church, find the world a madhouse and a madhouse home. Max the atheist sees things like Saint Thomas Aquinas, ranged, orderly, connected up." Tom, from his quirky private corner, sees the world's madness, Max, whose faith is in orderliness, cannot accommodate such a vision; his world is required to make sense. Prisoners or exiles like Dostoevski, Cervantes, and the two Thomas Mores have "seen visions, dreamed dreams," but "it is of no use in science unless you can measure it."

Earlier Max had "saved" Tom following his suicide attempt by naming his terror, "giving it habitation," knowing the worst of him and "naming it with ordinary words, English common nouns": Tom was having "troublesome mood swings," combined with "excellent insight." Now, as Tom speaks of "the soul of Western man," carelessly mentions the vines, and uses terms like angelism, Max the neobehaviorist is discomfited. "Belief. Truth values. These are relative things," goes the incantation by which he seeks to keep his world intact and banish the specter of the sniper and the conspiracy Tom has got wind of. On Tom's affair with Lola he says twice, "I am trying to see it as you see it," patronizing Tom's Catholicism. What worries Tom is that he feels no guilt, without which there can be no contrition or purpose of amendment and therefore no forgiveness of sin. Max wants to put Tom in a Skinner box and "condition away the contradiction" so he will never feel guilt. "Then I'd really be up the creek," Tom says, and Max repeats, somewhat despairingly, "I'm trying to see it."

Max cannot see it, of course. His mind is imprisoned in its own assumptions. His behaviorism cannot negotiate with other faiths; it can only fall back into the new mumbo jumbo: "Belief. Truth values. These are relative things." The reader who does not share Tom's Catholicism may be closer to Max's relativism, a sort of philosophical nowhere, but unless his imagination is too tightly bound he can share Tom's experience of events to come. And that imaginative element is important because the extent to which he participates will determine his response to the novel.

Much of the action now requires little explanation. Tom makes a visit to the Love Clinic, an elaborate sex research institute, and Percy's satire becomes rather broad as he gives us a multilayered scene with all sorts of absurdities taking place while the clinic's proudest exhibit, "Lonesome Lil," is dutifully masturbating beyond the viewing mirror. "Isn't it impolite not to watch her?" Tom wonders, his hand straying along the vaginal computer to touch fingers with Moira, one of his true loves. Father Kev Kevin, a liberal schismatic who is now chaplain to the clinic, sits at the vaginal console reading *Commonweal,* a lay Catholic periodical for which Percy has often written.

[Elsewhere] I spoke of the new Fall described in the novel. A sequence in this middle section of the novel shows the effects of this new Fall in a Southern context. Victor Charles appears to help when Tom passes out in a ditch near the animal shelter where Victor lives. Victor, whose loyalties are split between the black uprising and his ancient affection for Tom, warns Tom that he should move in with his mother. Something bad is going to happen. There is a scene illustrating the mutual concern and affection that often pervaded relations between white and black in the old days. Victor has returned from a remunerative job in Boston partly out of nostalgia for the old "shrimp jubilee," in which everybody—black and white—had spent the night on the beach catching shrimp by the light of gas lamps. Victor remembers Tom's family to one side of him and Leroy Ledbetter's to the other during one jubilee, a memory of olden days that is far more honest than the vision of Tara. Even now, Victor seems to have some feeling for Leroy, though Leroy now denies blacks entrance to his bar and helps keep them down. "It's so pitiful," Victor says. "You would think people with that much in common would want to save what they have."

A scene follows in which Percy describes a complicated breach of racial zoning that takes place in two seconds and brings the metallic taste of terror to Tom's throat. Tom recalls having tasted it after the Bantu uprising five years earlier when Leroy, then his partner in the Paradise Bowling Lanes, told him about the incident that triggered the uprising, Leroy's denial of an alley to a Bantu couple. Leroy is a seventh-generation Anglo-Saxon American like Tom, though "Protestant, countrified, sweet-natured," the sort who helps out when you have a flat tire. Then where does Tom's terror come from following the racial infraction?

> Not from the violence; violence gives release from terror. Not from Leroy's wrongness, for if he were altogether wrong, an evil man, the matter would be simple and no cause for terror. No, it came from Leroy's goodness, that he is a decent, sweet-natured man who would help out if you needed help, go out of his way and bind up a stranger's wounds. No, the terror comes from the goodness and what lies beneath, some fault in the soul's terrain so deep that all is well on top, evil grins like good, but something shears and tears deep down and the very ground stirs beneath one's feet.

What is terrifying is not the evil men of Hollywood legend, but the "good gone wrong and not knowing it," the "Southern sweetness and cruelty." That is what shakes Tom.

We are in territory occupied by the spirit of abstraction, that objectification of others, poisoned by resentment, that sees only abstractions or symbols in place of living individual humans. The "fault in the soul's terrain" is the rift in the humanity of men that is the modern Black Death, that malady no monkey knows, which has extended its sway even into the intimate Southern domain of the shrimp jubilee. In a remarkable passage that forms a centerpiece for Percy's comic synthesis, Tom sees a vision of the new Christ in his own reflection in the ancient pocked mirror behind the bar of the Little Napoleon:

> In the dark mirror there is a dim hollow-eyed Spanish Christ. The pox is spreading on his face. Vacuoles are opening in his chest. It is the new Christ, the spotted Christ, the maculate Christ, the sinful Christ. The old Christ died for our sins and it didn't work, we were not reconciled. The new Christ shall reconcile man with his sins. The new Christ lies drunk in a ditch. Victor Charles and Leroy Ledbetter pass by and see him. "Victor, do you love me?" "Sho, Doc." "Leroy, do you love me?" "Cut it out, Tom, you know better than to ask that." "Then y'all help me." "O.K., Doc." They laugh and pick up the new Christ, making a fireman's carry, joining four hands. They love the new Christ and so they love each other.

Undoubtedly some readers will see in this reflection the evidence that Tom More is the new Christ. I do not. The literary landscape is overpopulated with Christ figures, it seems to me, and it has become as difficult to circumvent as to create such symbols. Tom More is Tom More. What he sees in his own reflection is not himself as the new Christ but the *need* for a new Christ in a fantasy prompted by the racial predicament in which he finds himself.

In the limbo of chronic angelism-bestialism we find ourselves divided between our bestial impulses, which are fueled by hatred and violence, and our higher powers, which are stranded in abstract consciousness. One or the other normally predominates, but in either case our humanity, with its inwardness, is lost. So estranged do we become from each other—racially, socially, or personally—that we can relate to each other only through another we love. The old Christ is dead because we have become immune to the shining example; it cannot reconcile our angelic with our bestial selves. The new Christ lies drunk in a ditch. He needs us. He appeals to our love. Do you love me? Yes. "Then y'all help me." And in our love for him we unite our divided selves and join hands in the task.

This is well and good, you may say, for the South or for some small town or rural community where a few strands remain of the social fabric, but what of the anonymous North or the poor old polarized USA, where as in New York "life is simple, every man's your enemy, and you walk with your eyes straight ahead?" What would it take to work a similar effect? Is there anyone we all love? Walter Cronkite, perhaps, who has been with us on many a sad or happy occasion? Red Skelton, who has made us laugh?

When will the new Christ appear? Wait and watch, says Tom More; that is "the spirit of the new age." In the meantime we know how it stands with us, and Percy is surely right about the way of the new Christ: you touch people where they live, not where they do not.

The hottest political issue going, Tom has told us, is euthanasia, and a call on old Mr. Ives prepares the way for the grand finale of this section, Tom's trial in The Pit. In the opening pages we learned that the nation's number one killer, by authority of the Surgeon General's report, is "Senior Citizens' anomie," locally known as the "St. Petersburg blues." It strikes even at "Gerry Rehab," where old folks in perfect physical condition inexplicably grow sad, "sit slack and empty-eyed at shuffle board and ceramic oven" despite the opportunity to develop their "creative and altruistic potential." Mr. Ives, "a little bald-headed monkey of a man" from Tennessee whose eyes "fairly hop with—what? rage or risibility?" has been seen to "expose himself and defecate on Flirtation Walk." Worse yet, this overgarrulous man has gone mute. The diagnosis is "senile psychopathy and mutism," and unless Tom can save him, Mr. Ives is clearly slated for the "Happy Isles," meaning the "Permanent Separation Center" and the "Euphoric On-Switch" in a Georgia town appropriately called Jekyl.

The lapsometer reveals a furious redness in his red nucleus. Mr. Ives is "too damn mad to talk," Tom says; he trusts no one. A reading at Brodmann 28, the locus of concrete memory, shows a merry swing of the needle when Tom reminds him of their playing checkers together in his camper ten years ago on just such summer evenings. As yet Tom can only diagnose with the lapsometer, and he cannot prove anything even in diagnosis; but armed with his knowledge of Mr. Ives's condition he is better prepared for his trial-by-combat with Buddy Brown in The Pit, where the old man's fate is to be decided.

It is at this point that Percy's Mephistophilis appears in the person of Art Immelmann. He arrives, like Marlowe's figure, amid thunder, as Tom More sits in his office listening to Don Giovanni begin his descent into hell: "A bolt of lightning strikes a transformer with a great crack. Sparks fly. The ox-lot is filled with a rinsing blue-white light. Trees jump backward. The lights go out." Unlike Marlowe's Mephistophilis, Immelmann is not invoked by Tom, the Dr. Faustus of this piece, but intrudes himself like an unwelcome drug salesman. In the lightning flames he "seems to come forward by jumps" with his big attaché case, shouting over the storm: "Funding is my game." Curiously old-fashioned with his flat-top haircut and white shirt, he looks like a "small-town businessman in the old Auto Age" but speaks the dialect of "one of those liaison fellows from Washington," as he presents himself, moving between the big foundations in the private sector and the National Institute of Mental Health. Immelmann has come to confer recognition on Tom's success in developing a technique that "maximizes and unites hardware and software capabilities," a "tool for dealing with the heretofore immeasurable and intangible stresses that are rending the national fabric." Percy gives the devil the best lines as Immelmann proceeds in the sophisticated lingo of the funding game to describe the lapsometer—the key to Percy's synthesis—as a tool "operative at behavioral, political, and philosophical levels." The people he represents are ready, as we might expect, to "fund an interdisciplinary task force and implement a crash program" to provide every physician and scientist in the country with a MOQUOL within a year's time.

A perfect tempter, offering just what the object of his designs wants and hopes for. He has even brought a contract transferring patent rights that he urges Tom to sign: standard procedure for any contract with the "private sector." Victory, Tom thinks, recalling his uncle's advice to "guard against the sadness of hubris." There is no doubt that Tom stands in peril, with his longings for the Nobel Prize, though he is not at this time in the market for voluptuousness; he already has Moira and Lola, not to speak of Ellen and Hester waiting in the wings. He is not trying to sell his soul but to donate his lapsometer. And who knows but that even Dr. Faustus, if Mephistophilis had spoken the language of "multilevel capacity" and "built-in logistical factors," might have sent him back to hell empty-handed? In any case, Tom declines the offer to sign over his patent rights; and Art—it seems fitting that a contemporary Mephistophilis should be known by his first name—leaves by the back door, perhaps taking the short cut to the old Southern Hotel. But how would he know about the short cut? Tom wonders, and Percy ends the July First section on that mystifying note.

In the brief section of July Second, Property Rights Sunday is being celebrated in the Catholic Church. Monsignor Schleifkopf, whose name means Knothead, preaches about those two fellow property owners, Joseph of Arimathea and Lazarus: "Dearly Beloved: we are reminded by the best commentators that Lazarus was not a poor man, that he lived comfortably in a home that he owned." Tom's Mother, Marva, a "realtor" who no doubt calls a house a "home," lives comfortably in her own physical habitation. "She sparkles with good health and is at one with herself." She is something of a prophetess, having predicted "four out of the last five assassinations," and is likewise immersed in astrology. She cautions Tom, who is a Cancer and therefore "deeply sensitive," to beware of Aries and Libra. (Ellen is evidently an Aries, and Moira, "that little Left snippet," a Libra.) The perfect match would be a Taurus—namely Lola—who by good fortune also stands to inherit Tara. Marva has a misty faith in the land: "Do you remember what Scarlett said about the land? Or was it in *The Good Earth?*" "Yes," says Dusty Rhoades, whose faith is a drier one. Marva's religion is a marshy compound of real estate and the occult, overlain by a shroud of Christianity. Wet or dry, Knothead faith is intimately bound to property.

Far closer to the faith of Christ is the unlikely love couple from the swamp who chanced upon a Confederate Bible, "read it as if it had never been read before, the wildest unlikeliest doctrine imaginable, believed it, decided to be married and baptize their children." As Sutter Vaught wrote in his casebook, "There is after all something worse than being God-forsaken. It is when God overstays his welcome and takes up with the wrong people." Kierkegaard wondered how to introduce Christianity into Danish Christendom; how would Christ find entrance to Paradise Estates? By surprise, perhaps, through the naïveté of a love couple in the swamp, who take a fresh look at his story and catch at least a glimpse of what is there.

Finally the big day arrives, the day on which Tom is to meet Buddy Brown in The Pit. On his way to an appointment with the Director he runs into Buddy, who greets him with a pinch and a wink. "Son, this time I got you by the short hairs," says Buddy, a licentious man who keeps himself exceptionally clean. Now Buddy runs through the secular litany referred to earlier as Tom listens like Binx Bolling enduring his Aunt Emily:

> "It's the quality of life that counts."
> "Yes."
> "And the right of the individual to control his own body."
> "Well—"
> "And above all a man's sacred right to choose his own destiny and realize his own potential."
> "Well—"
> "Would you let your own mother suffer?"
> "Yes."
> "I don't believe you. I know you too well and know that you place a supreme value on human values."
> "Yes."
> "We believe in the same things, differing only in the best way to achieve them."

The comedy of this scene arises from the incoherence of the consensus anthropology, which suddenly becomes apparent. In the mouth of Buddy Brown, who has already made up his mind to ship Mr. Ives off to be executed, this talk of "a man's sacred right to choose his own destiny and realize his own potential" rings with mockery, but Buddy would be the last to detect it. The final line could be translated, "We're not really sure what we believe, so let's not quarrel, let's just do it my way." Buddy speaks a language of ideals drawn from the Judaeo-Christian tradition and operates on behaviorist assumptions. "It is the job of the satirist," Percy says, "to detect these slips and to exaggerate them so that they become known to everybody."

The prelude to The Pit is Tom's visit to the Director. He enters as a patient, having forgotten that Monday is patients' day. Tom's hope is that the Director will help him secure funds to develop the lapsometer. Though the Director, as a behaviorist, is unlikely to smile on the notion of an ontological lapsometer, he is also dying of cancer. "A dying king, said Sir Thomas More, is apt to be wiser than a healthy king. A dying behaviorist may be a good behaviorist." But as it turns out, the Director patronizes Tom about the twenty-five million dollars he needs, reminding him of his "patient-staff status." The precarious balance of Tom's status is pivotal to the scene as he tips more and more in the direction of patient. The Director enjoins him to "hang in right where you are." Then, as the lapsometer lies on the desk between them "like a dog turd," he asks Tom: "Do you think you are well?" No, Tom says, seeing no particular connection between his answer and the merit of his proposal. But at the Director's "Well—?" his balance tilts: "My God, he's right. $25,000,000. An ontological lapsometer. I'm mad as a hatter." The Director inquires ironically about the lapse measured by the lapsometer: "A fall perhaps from a state of innocence?" whereupon Tom withdraws defeated, wanting to practice medicine from his bed on the ward, "lie happy and stiff on my bed, like a Hindoo on his bed of nails, and treat sane folk and sane doctors from the sane world, which is the maddest world of all." He is now so addled that he cannot speak coherently to his nemesis, Buddy Brown. "I do not speak well. I've lost. I'm a patient."

It is in this condition that he signs away his patent rights to Art Immelmann. The stage on which Percy's Faustus meets his Mephistophilis is the men's room, where this emissary from the dark regions of "funding" is in his element. A bit earlier Art has identified himself as a coordinator, not the man with the big ideas like Tom, just a "tinkerer." Now he says obscenely, "Let me see your MOQUOL." He informs Tom how he can turn the lapsometer from diagnosis to treatment, and he tells Tom what he wants to hear in Tom's own private language. Like the diabolical figure who accompanies Hawthorne's young Goodman Brown through the forest, he has the gift of "discoursing so aptly that his arguments [seem] rather to spring up in the bosom of his auditor than to be suggested by himself." Tom wonders how a man who looks like "the sort of fellow who used to service condom vendors in the old Auto Age" can know these things, but to his doubts Art replies, "Drink this drink and you'll never want a drink."

Tom drinks it, of course. Having himself been massaged by his own lapsometer, his terror now gone and his large bowel "slack as a string, clear as a bell," he signs the contract. His wishes are fulfilled. "Now you can use your talents for the good of mankind and the increase of knowledge," Art says, deftly touching the scientist's pride. "All you have to do is never look back and never be sorry as per agreement." Tom seems to have closed a better deal than did Faustus, who promised never to think on God:

> Nor will Faustus henceforth. Pardon him for this,
> And Faustus vows never to look to heaven!
> Never to name God or to pray to Him,
> To burn His Scriptures, slay His ministers,
> And make my spirits pull His churches down.

During this scene in the men's room Percy does something highly unusual. Art turns the lapsometer on Tom, and the effects are given phenomenologically. First Tom's anxiety level is raised until he feels "the Terror, but tolerable." He sees the wall urinals as "shaped like skulls." A "minus-seven Chloride dose" brings a dramatic effect: "Something in my diaphragm lets go. I realize I've been breathing at the top of my lungs for forty-five years." Then he notices his hand, a beautiful strong hand, but the hand of a stranger: "How can a man spend forty-five years as a stranger to himself? No other creature would do such a thing. No animal would, for he is pure organism. No angel would, for he is pure spirit." When a person is reconciled with himself and thus united as man-spirit, the author seems to be suggesting, he will experience his hand not as Roquentin does in Sartre's *Nausea*—as an alien fat-bellied crab lying on its back—but as a strangely beautiful manifestation of being.

Percy then goes beyond this in the attempt to convey something extremely difficult to grasp. Art stimulates Brodmann 11, "the area of the musical-erotic." "Here the abstract is experienced concretely and the concrete abstractly." One loves a woman, for example, "both in herself and insofar as she is a woman," faithlessly and yet, as one loves music, truly. "A woman is the concrete experienced abstractly, as women." The love one experiences in this realm is that of the "scientist-lover," Art explains, and has its counterpart in scientific knowledge, which is "neutral morally, abstractive and godlike." Tom hears the "love music of man in particular for women in general" and the concept is translated into experiential terms as he begins murmuring to himself:

> Who am I?
> I am he who loves. I am in love. I love.
> Who do you love?
> You.
> Who is "you"?
> A girl.
> What girl?
> Any girl you please. You.

Is this revelation that we find here, genuine insight, or the delusion of one who attempts, as Marlowe put it, to "practice more than heavenly power permits"?

The question is not easily resolved. One clue lies in the fact that the devil again has the best answers. Art insinuates himself into Tom's thoughts to get him to sign the contract: "Isn't it better to feel good rather than bad?" "Yes." "Isn't it better to be happy than unhappy?" "Yes." Who can dispute such arguments? The limitations of such reasoning are those of the musical-erotic, a term of Kierkegaard's that represents the highest achievement of the aesthetic sphere. Seen from the aesthetic sphere, the musical-erotic is the best of the good; seen from the ethical sphere, it is bad. Don Juan is the personification of the musical-erotic, which in its immediacy can only be expressed in music, and it does not carry the connotations we attach to sensuality but is translated simply as "sensuousness—an amoral wild impulse following its purely natural urge." That is its beauty and the upper boundary of its possibilities.

The public trial of Tom More culminates in the splendid comic uproar of The Pit. Sir Thomas More refused allegiance to the new order and was tried and beheaded for his crime. Tom's trial is a little different. He too refuses allegiance to the new order, in this case a neobehaviorist order descended from B. F. Skinner, but he is not beheaded. His trial consists of gladiatorial combat with one of Skinner's intellectual heirs for the life of poor old Mr. Ives—in The Pit, where Tom's assumptions and those of the behaviorists can be put to the empirical test. Is man simply an organism to be controlled and treated by proper conditioning, a mere piano key, or is he that testy and paradoxical being who emerged from Dostoevski's underground to proclaim his freedom and boast of his bad liver? Can he find breathing space in the new Crystal Palace of the behaviorists or will he smash the windows in search of open sky?

Tom enters The Pit a decided underdog in the contest, having been reduced to "patient" status, though after a MOQUOL massage by Art Immelmann his heart is full of love and his mind "like a meat grinder ready to receive the raw stuff of experience and turn out neat pattycake principles." The steep slopes of the amphitheater are jammed with students, who—like students in general, Tom thinks—are a scurvy lot, half of them anti-euthanasics who revere Dr. Spiro T. Agnew, the other half "qualitarians" following Hesse, Skinner, and Justice William O. Douglas, who has presided over a hundred million abortions in India and an equal number of "painless 'terminations' of miserable and unproductive old folk." As Buddy Brown and Tom square off in this strange court a tacit behaviorist assumption emerges that Mr. Ives is guilty of terminal failure to respond successfully to conditioning and that unless Tom, upon whom the burden of proof rests, can somehow exonerate him, Mr. Ives is necessarily to be shipped off to a painless termination.

Buddy Brown leads off with his "differential diagnosis: advanced atherosclerosis, senile psychosis, psychopathic and antisocial behavior, hemiplegia and aphasia following a cerebrovascular accident." Solid medical evidence from an expert, by the sound of it. Meanwhile Tom idles away his time admiring the beauty of his hand. Buddy omits to make a therapeutic recommendation; it scarcely seems necessary. "We are still waiting for your diagnosis, Dr. More," he says with the gentleness of victory. "I found no significant pathology," Tom replies, recommending that Mr. Ives be discharged. The conflict builds itself into the scene quoted [elsewhere] with Tom uttering the word *funeral* and the girls pulling their skirts down over their knees as the Director warns Tom to watch what he says. Mr. Ives's "bright monkey eyes" begin to snap. "I repeat," Tom says to the back rows. "If Mr. Ives is going to be referred to the Happy Isles of Georgia, which is nothing but a euthanasia facility, he has the right to know it and to prepare himself accordingly. And he has the right to know who his executioner is."

The Director threatens to send Tom back to the ward and Tom wonders if in fact that is where he belongs, but Buddy Brown saves him by forcibly giving him an alcohol test and pronouncing him "drunk as a lord!" Tom reacts by inhibiting Buddy's inhibitory centers with the lapsometer, confident that it will be enough just to "let Buddy be what he is." Buddy begins making lewd half-audible remarks and Tom moves on to Mr. Ives, further scandalizing the behaviorists with his metaphysics. "What is interesting [in Mr. Ives]," he says, "is the structure of his selfhood as it relates both to his fellow seniors in the Tampa settlement and to the scientists here." Let him speak if he is well, the students clamor. The lapsometer now comes to the rescue. Tom administers a "light Chloride dampening" to the red nucleus of Mr. Ives and a "moderate Sodium massage" to his speech area. Mr. Ives begins to speak in a "deep drawling voice." The flavor of his remarks in the dramatic moments that follow emerges in his answer to the Director's query as to why he had behaved so outrageously to his fellow "retirees": "Doctor, how would you like it if during the most critical time of your experiments with the Skinner box that won you the Nobel Prize, you had been pestered without letup by a bunch of chickenshit Ohioans?" His explanation for not having walked or spoken for a month resounds with contempt: "There is only one kind of response to those who would control your responses by throwing you in a Skinner box," and that is to "refuse to respond at all." Tom recommends the old man be released and furnished with transportation back to Tennessee, where Mr. Ives's subsequent plans sound remarkably similar to sentiments expressed elsewhere by Tom: "Write a book, look at the hills, live till I die."

It is a superlatively funny scene and succeeds in discrediting behaviorist assumptions. The consensus anthropology is exposed as a fraud. Tom the underdog comes out on top and the whole circus disintegrates into farce as Art Immelmann, who has somehow got hold of Tom's box of lapsometers— "Now what the devil is he doing?" Tom wonders—proceeds to distribute them to one and all. Without a "pilot," he explains, they cannot hope to "go national": "That's boilerplate, Doc." Notwithstanding its dangers, the lapsometer proves a smashing success for Ted and Tanya, who are successfully interacting on the floor beneath the seats. "All we feared was fear itself," they chorus as he steps over them with a gentlemanly "Pardon." The libido of even the glacial Presbyterian Ellen threatens to break loose. "Did I say it aloud?" she asks Tom. And off they go, Tom between Max and Ellen, as the Director discovers how fair a fair youth can be, misquoting from the classics to a "handsome peach-faced lad" from an old-line Southern family.

THE TEMPTATION OF TOM MORE

Sir Thomas More stood his ground good-humoredly and was beheaded, later to be canonized a saint. It is difficult to foresee any such clear prospect for Tom at this hour of his triumph. Superficially he seems in little danger of hubris, with his manifold weaknesses and ailments and his three girls, heading into a Fourth of July on which his lapsometers are scattered over the landscape and he is being hunted by the same Bantus who aim to kidnap the Christian Kaydettes. On the other hand, as Tom himself might say, never have fame and power hovered so near. Students have applauded him, his girls are brimming with admiration, even the Director is now eager to get him under contract before MIT or Harvard latches onto him. And always, in the wings waiting, there is Art Immelmann, with his access to funds and high-powered committees. Tom has emerged victorious from his public trial; now he must face the deadlier temptations of hubris in the privacy of his mind.

The action in this second Fourth of July section centers on the hijinks of revolution and Tom's love tryst with his three girls in the broken-down Howard Johnson's, most of it good fun that breaks again and again into burlesque, at times threatening to become tiresome. But underlying all the funny business are the Faustus theme and a religious theme involving Samantha that is virtually unseen and yet emerges almost inexplicably from time to time. The death of Tom's daughter Samantha is the tragic face beneath the comic mask of Tom More. We have seen how well he can diagnose the ills of others. Now we have a chance to see how well he perceives his own, as within the panoramic public scene of the novel the private ordeal of its narrator now begins to put forth a subdued light that comes to suffuse and illumine the wider sphere.

It was the ghastly death of Samantha that put Tom on the skids some eight years earlier. She had been the cement holding his life together. Her death gave him an excuse to drink and go into decline. As his intelligence became more and more "duly darkened," he became mired deeper and deeper in the comic religious state in which he still lives, saying the right thing and doing the wrong. The religious theme surfaces more and more as memories of Samantha and Doris are prompted by events.

As Tom leaves his house on this "hot still gold-green Fourth of July" the sight of P. T. Bledsoe's house burning cheerfully and unattended in the middle of Paradise Estates recalls to him how thirty years earlier, as a thirteen-year-old, he had "defiled himself" in the skeletal bathroom of the house, then under construction, amid the carpenter's litter of copper flashing and blocks of wood, "man's excellent geometries wrought from God's somewhat lumpish handiwork." A buzz on the Anser-Phone in his shirt pocket feels like a heart attack and produces "belated contrition": "God, don't let me die. I haven't lived, and there's the summer ahead and music and science and girls."

While he waits for Moira to shower during their rendezvous at Howard Johnson's, Tom drinks a toddy and recalls his lost life with Doris in the old Auto Age before Samantha was born. Doris had never understood why he would leave her in the motel Sundays, during their travels, and find his way to mass in some nearby church. The passage is revealing:

> Now here was the strangest exercise of all! Leaving the coordinate of the motel at the intersection of the interstates, leaving the motel with standard doors and carpets and plumbing, leaving the interstates extending infinitely in all directions, abscissa and ordinate, descending through a moonscape countryside to a —town! Where people had been living all these years, and to some forlorn little mass, stepping up on the porch as if I had been doing it every Sunday for the past twenty years, and here comes the stove-up bemused priest with his cup (what am I doing out here? says his dazed expression) upon whose head hands had been laid and upon this other head other hands and so on, for here off I-51 I touched the thread in the labyrinth.

The labyrinth, it becomes clear in the context of the novel, is the abstract "moonscape" terrain of modern urban society, this nowhere of which Binx Bolling has such a fear, with its interstates and standardized motels set down indiscriminately in the "green hills of Tennessee or out in haunted New Mexico." The thread in this labyrinth is the "forlorn" little church in a real town where people "had been living all these years," a concrete link with time and place, and the "stove-up bemused priest" upon whose head "hands had been placed."

Tom cannot say whether his exhilaration comes from "eating Christ" or from his "secret discovery of the singular thread" in this "geometry of Holiday Inns and improbable interstates," but the feeling seems to spring from the weird conjunction of terrain abstracted right out of time and a real place with ties going back, back, back. The experience is an existential repetition that enjoys the surprise of a rotation—suddenly out of the twilit labyrinth of the Eclipse, a thread leading all the way back to the Event. Doris, "being spiritual and seeing religion as spirit," could never understand "that it took religion to save me from the spirit world, from orbiting the earth like Lucifer and the angels, that it took nothing less than touching the thread off the misty interstates and eating Christ himself to make me mortal man again and let me inhabit my own flesh and love her in the morning." Now he has lost the thread and is himself lost in the labyrinth.

It was with Samantha that Tom used to go to mass on summer evenings, and now, as he carries on the tryst with Moira, the ghost of Samantha keeps coming back. It is her ghost that keeps a few embers alive in him. Moira is an empty-headed romantic caught in the common snares of inauthenticity. She asks naïvely, "Could we live in Paradise?" Tom carries her in his arms "like a child" and pats her "just as I used to pat Samantha when she had growing pains." Moira, while sharing in his fling, thus keeps fanning the embers of his memory. She plugs a quarter into the vibrating bed just as Samantha used to do. Her prodigality with her charms prompts an angry memory of the time Samantha was stood up by a boy from St. Aloysius: "Curse God, curse the nuns for arranging the dance, goddamn the little Celt-Catholic bastards, little Mediterranean lowbrow French-dago jerks. Anglo-Saxon Presbyterians would have better manners even if they didn't believe in God." The memory calls up tears, bringing Tom closer to a recognition of his present state, and he feels guilt for accepting Moira's favors while she holds herself so cheap. "With her I feel like a man watching a child run around with a forty-carat diamond. Her casualness with herself makes me sweat."

The adventure with Moira is a rotation leading nowhere. Tom's dalliance in the bunker with Lola had been a rotation too, as he could not make his mother understand: "A perfect encounter, but it is not to be thought that we could repeat it." But in promoting, with the aid of Dusty Rhoades, Tom's marriage to Lola, Marva is trying to propel him into the fake repetition of life at Tara. He is tempted by Lola's vision of him as "an agreeable H. G. Wells nineteenth-century scientist type, 'doing my researches' in the handsome outhouse of Tara"—the same kind of researches, incidentally, that Aunt Emily had foreseen for Binx. "Come back to Tara," Lola begs him. "Come back and put down roots with Lola." But even the music of this idyll, "happy old Haydn, whose music does not brook one single shadow of sadness," now seems to belong more to Vince Marsaglia, the gangster who had bought Tara from M-G-M, than to Tom More. When Tom says to Lola, "I've told you we can't go back to Tara," he is doing more than echoing Thomas Wolfe. The mossy image of Tara is Percy's best lampoon of Southern sentimentality. The roads to Tara are dusty with the tramp of antebellum feet.

Tom's road to salvation takes another route, but first some other matters need attending to. He is taken captive by Uru and Victor, who drive him through Paradise in an armored golf cart and imprison him in Monsignor Schleifkopf's office. Tom escapes through the air-conditioning vent, removing the screws from the grill with the "proper bronze sword" of the "somewhat prissy bronze archangel" Saint Michael—saved, this bad Catholic of the subtitle, by his knowledge of the sword, which he used "to fiddle with during the Holy Name meetings." It was Saint Michael, we might recall, who led Adam and Eve out of Paradise after the Fall, while the "brandished sword of God before them blazed." Tom leaves Paradise in a wild burlesque, setting off the carillon chimes, discarding Saint Michael's sword at the outside grill, kicking the grill loose during the major chord of "White Christmas," and coming out "feet-first, born again, ejected into the hot bright perilous world" of the Fourth of July, whereupon Lola rescues him on horseback and the two of them ride off on a mare called Yellow Rose while the carillon sounds "The First Noel" and Victor Charles exhorts Tom to "take care this little lady." "Isn't Victor wonderful!" Lola cries, catching a glimpse of old-time ways. "Tom, let's go to Tara!" But Tom, preferring moonscape to mold, directs her to Howard Johnson's instead.

Returning to the Love Clinic to retrieve Lola's cello, Tom learns he is being credited with a "breakthrough." At "Love" they have "implemented" his insight that "marital love often founders on boredom and the struggle to attain a theoretical orgasmic perfection" and with consummate imagination are making a "fresh start" with "substitute partners." In this scene Percy finally satirizes the misuse of the word *existential*: "Oh dear!" Father Kev Kevin cries, watching Stryker lead Helga into the Observer Stimulation Overflow Area. "If ever there was an existential decision—!"

A conversation in this scene between Tom and Art Immelmann suggests how one form of the monstrousness of our century is born of the rift in man's nature that Percy describes. Tom warns Art of the danger of applying the lapsometer to the "prefrontal abstractive centers" of a man: "It would render him totally abstracted from himself, totally alienated from the concrete world, and in such a state of angelism that he will fall prey to the first abstract notion proposed to him and will kill anybody who gets in his way, torture, execute, wipe out entire populations, all with the best possible motives and the best possible intentions, in fact in the name of peace and freedom, etcetera." Art's diabolic response to the horror of this vision is a delighted: "Yeah, Doc! Your MOQUOL surpasses my most sanguine expectations."

What Tom describes in his warning is not altogether new. Consider the dream Raskolnikov has at the conclusion of *Crime and Punishment*:

> While sick, he had dreamed the whole world was condemned to suffer a terrible, unprecedented, and unparalleled plague, which had spread to Europe from the depths of Asia. Except for a small handful of the chosen, all were doomed to perish. A new kind of trichinae had appeared, microscopic substances that lodged in men's bodies. Yet these were spiritual substances as well, endowed with mind and will. Those infected were seized immediately and went mad. Yet people never considered themselves so clever and so unhesitatingly right as these infected ones considered themselves. Never had they considered their decrees, their

scientific deductions, their moral convictions and their beliefs
more firmly based. Whole settlements, whole cities and nations,
were infected and went mad.

The affinity is apparent, though where Dostoevski is giving us a vision of
future horrors Percy is trying to account for those already in evidence. With
chronic angelism-bestialism man's essential humanity is divided between angelic and bestial elements, and he has little defense against the impulses that
assail him. A vacuum will be filled. "War," as Percy said, "is better than
nothing." The effect may be worse when the motive force is an angelic
dedication to abstract ideals than when it springs directly from the most
bestial of hatreds. In either case the spirit of abstraction is at work and the
price is paid by concrete human beings living in the world.

   The only real immunization against such viruses is a truly human condition, man united with himself. How can the rift be healed? The novel,
which was originally entitled *How to Make Love in the Ruins,* suggests
possibilities. We learned from Kirkegaard that the "crowd" infected by these
plagues is made up of individuals, and we have one such individual before
us, Tom More. Now that we know the doctor's diagnosis of the others, we
can return to how it is with him.

   To Art's trumpeting that he has "already elicited positive interactions
from both ends of the spectrum" with the lapsometer, Tom breaks in: "Goddamn, man, do you realize what you're saying?" Art winces at the mention
of God, but to Tom's "Get out of my way" this satanic figure resorts to his
old bag of tricks, mentioning Tom's prospect of winning the Nobel Prize,
which leaves Tom with a "pleasant tingle" running across the sacrum. Later,
Tom's allegation that "you and your goddamn foundations" are somehow
responsible for what is happening, Art winces again and denies on principle
that they "do" anything to anyone. "We only help people do what they want
to do," he protests in a classic disclaimer of moral responsibility. "We facilitate social interaction in order to isolate factors." And here Percy has the
devil himself quoting scripture in proclaiming that his people are "dedicated
to the freedom of the individual to choose his own destiny and develop his
own potential." Hearing this pious claim from such a source, we should
question it from anyone whose loyalties belong to other regions.

   It is hardly surprising that Tom finally conquers his own hubris in the
form of a plush post in Denmark in which to await his Nobel Prize. What
is interesting is how he does it and why. It may be his invocation of Sir
Thomas More that drives Immelmann hence, but what prompts him to resist
in the first place? Neither a mechanical necessity of the plot, I think, nor the

demands of any mythic or literary parallel outside the book, but the terms the author has set up within the novel: Tom's need to escape More's syndrome and to live as a human. Religion is instrumental, and in Tom's labyrinth the one remaining thread is his memory of Samantha.

The key scene is a flashback, triggered evidently by Uru's rejection of Tom's goodwill blessing with a final: "You better go back, Doc, while you can." Tom does go back, in memory, to the day when he had stood by Samantha's bed. She asks, "Papa, have you lost your faith? No, he says.

> "Then why don't you go to Mass any more?"
> "I don't know. Maybe because you don't go with me."
> "Papa, you're in greater danger than Mama."
> "How is that?"
> "Because she is protected by Invincible Ignorance."
> "That's true," I said, laughing.
> "She doesn't know any better."
> "She doesn't."
> "You do."
> "Yes."
> "Just promise me one thing, Papa."
> "What's that?"
> "Don't commit the one sin for which there is no forgiveness."
> "Which one is that?"
> "The sin against grace. If God gives you the grace to believe in him and love him and you refuse, the sin will not be forgiven you."

This sin against grace can no doubt be interpreted in strictly Catholic terms. But the novel goes beyond any sectarian confines to attempt a synthesis of religious and secular thought, and grace here has another dimension. What forms of grace are open to Tom More and to the rest of us who are exiled to the postmodern world?

Here again, I think, as in *The Last Gentleman,* grace is subjectivity or inwardness. The thread in Tom's labyrinth is the memory of Samantha, which has become the only link with his former faith. The sinful condition in which he lives is the opposite of faith. But the grace of inwardness can be viewed secularly as well. In the grip of the malaise we become lost in a limbo of objectivity. We have a clue to what grace might be in another memory of Samantha. Tom's heart was broken by her death. While she lived, "life still had its same peculiar tentativeness, people living as usual by fits and starts, aiming and missing, while present time went humming"; but even then he had foreknowledge that "the second she died, remorse would come and give time its bitter specious wholeness. If only—If only we hadn't been defeated by humdrum humming present time and missed it, missed ourselves, missed everything." In the limbo of the malaise, present time defeats us. To catch it might be, as Chuck Parker says, to live "completely and in the moment the way the prothonotary warbler lives flashing holy fire." Or better still, to reenter paradise and live there "both as man and spirit, whole and intact man-spirit, as solid flesh as a speckled trout, a dappled thing, yet aware of itself as a self!"

The memory of Samantha pulls Tom out of his abstracted orbit and gives him access to his own inwardness, where he is whole and intact. In the illumination of his reviving faith his condition becomes apparent to him and he realizes he has been feasting on Samantha's death. When he had refused to take her to Lourdes, Doris, who though a dumbbell knew how to read his faults, saw that he refused in fear the girl might be cured. "What then? Suppose you ask God for a miracle and God says yes, very well. How do you live the rest of your life?" How indeed? Who can shoulder such a load? And with that recognition Tom leaves the realm of the comic religious, where he knows without doing, and resumes a life of doing as he knows.

The Samantha theme now recedes and Percy returns to Faustus. Recognizing what is working below the surface, we know that the actual spurning of Art's offer is a very minor victory. The scene itself is comical. "Our work here is finished," the novel's Mephistophilis remarks, gazing happily at the smoking bunker, in an echo of the concluding note of *The Tempest*. He manifests an evil influence over Tom, advancing lapsometer in hand. Tom cannot move from the spot. He peers through the smoke at his adversary, who declares: "The two of you will have to come," "If we both go, Chief," Ellen says in something like a farewell to the Garden, "maybe it will be all right." "We'll all be happy in Copenhagen," Art murmurs, breaking into song: *"Beautiful beautiful Copenhagen."* Then, echoing Helga of the Love Clinic with a "Let's go, kids," he touches Ellen, at which Tom closes his eyes and offers a good prayer, for a bad Catholic: *"Sir Thomas More, kinsman, saint, best dearest merriest of Englishmen, pray for us and drive this son of a bitch hence."* Opening his eyes, he finds Art "turning slowly away, wheeling in slow motion, a dazed hurt look through the eyes as if he had been struck across the face." Unlike Faustus, Tom had never sworn not to invoke the name of God or his representatives, and Art Immelmann is powerless against Tom's kinsman saint. The innocent Ellen feels sorry for Art as he vanishes into the smoke. The July action of the novel closes with Ellen smoothing Tom's eyebrows with her spit and urging that the two of them go home.

EAST OF THE NEW EDEN

The epilogue opens on a note of reconciliation. The mood is pastoral, and the change in Tom's life is nowhere better conveyed than in this passage worthy of Thoreau at his best: "Water is the mystical element! At dawn the black bayou breathes a white vapor. The oars knock, cypress against cypress, but the sound is muffled, wrapped in cotton. As the trotline is handed along, the bank quickly disappears and the skiff seems to lift and be suspended in a new element globy and white. Silence presses in and up from the vaporish depths come floating great green turtles, blue catfish, lordly gaspergous." Our strivings now are ended, the tone seems to say. Life begins. The mood belongs to merry England, not the aspiring Elizabethan mood of Marlowe's *Doctor Faustus* but the quiet contentment he voices in "The Passionate Shepherd to His Love":

> Come live with me and be my love,
> And we will all the pleasures prove
> That valleys, groves, hills, and fields,
> Woods, or steepy mountain yields.

Five years have passed, enough for an age. "Now while you work, you also watch and listen and wait. In the last age we planned projects and cast ahead of ourselves." No more. Tom is reconciled at last, this time to himself. "All any man needs," he says, "is time and desire and the sense of his own sovereignty."

The externals underlying this transformation are evident enough. He now occupies the slave quarters because the Bantus have won—not by force of arms but by oil money—and in a reversal of roles have taken over Paradise while Tom hoes collards in a more humble garden. Tom's showdown with Art Immelmann evidently failed to curb his ambition; he sank all his money into the lapsometer and it was insolvency, not broken pride, that brought out his humility. The aspiration symbolized by the lapsometer was one to "practice more than heavenly power permits," and we knew all along it would have to be duly chastened. The Bantus, on the other hand, are riding high, and a good share of the epilogue elaborates the old notion that the more it changes the more it stays the same. Colley Wilkes, the "super-Bantu" Tom had diagnosed years before as "a self successfully playing at being a self that is not itself," counsels patience in the face of the discrimination Tom encounters from the Bantu medical society. "These things take time," his wife explains. The "Troubles" five years earlier, Colley remarks with equanimity, were the usual thing: "People resorting to violence instead of using democratic processes to resolve their differences."

If the lapsometer fails to effect a miracle cure in Tom's life, as we knew it would, he has nevertheless stumbled upon a simple and ancient remedy. His housing suggests its nature. He no longer lives in the luxury of a mock-Paradise or visits run-down motels with three beloveds, which is to say none; instead he lives in the Slave Quarters with Ellen. Back in the old Howard Johnson's her virtue had been almost oppressive, and throughout the novel she has been Tom's Girl Friday, faithful to "Chief," joining in his triumphs and misfortunes. Now it seems fitting that the "ripe Georgia persimmon not a peach" should share his new quarters in a sort of modified intersubjective communion. I say *modified* because in this novel perfection is not yet in evidence. There is a good deal of plain old English-style muddling through. When Tom goes to confession for the first time in eleven years the best he can do is feel sorry he feels no sorrow for the sins he confesses, though he willingly puts on the sackcloth as penance. A tolerant fellow, he mixes easily with love couples and Bantus as well as Presbyterians. Having escaped the false paradise of the New Eden, he tends collards in a small plot to the east while his less-innocent Eve stirs grits in the kitchen.

The outcome of Tom's private ordeal casts a light over the public landscape of the novel, but Percy does not presume to edify. Nor can the novel be construed as a defense of a Christian life. "To defend anything is always to discredit it," Kierkegaard wrote. The joyous tone of the epilogue speaks for itself. The consensus anthropology is revealed in The Pit as a fraud, but Percy does not insist the reader accept his own view of man. His comic synthesis will stand on either religious or secular premises. More's syndrome holds for both.

The novel offers another form of grace to its readers: the author's comic therapy. There is a connection, after all, between humor and wholeness. Whose ox has not been gored in this book? I doubt that anyone can read it without taking offense. But in the divided state of angelism-bestialism, humor can heal; it offers release from the grip of bestial aggressions even while restoring moral perspective. The comic is just what Emerson called it: "a pledge of sanity," the "balance-wheel" of the intellect. With the spirit of abstraction rampant in our society, humor may be the only release from collective madness. It plays such a key role in *Love in the Ruins* that the novel's theme could be given in a paraphrase of the scientist's prayer: "Lord, grant that we be delivered from the Black Death and find ourselves in our love for You. Failing that, Lord, grant that we recover our humanity in loving and being true to one other. Failing that, Lord, grant us at least the power to stand back and see the humor of our predicament before it all collapses around our ears."

The novel ends hopefully, on Christmas Eve. "Barbecuing in my sackcloth," Tom says, opening the final section with a perfect tonal marriage of penance and celebration. He sneaks a few drinks of Early Times and goes in to carry Ellen, a "noble, surprisingly heavy, Presbyterian armful," to her new king-sized bed. Even the ivy imagery, which up until now has been identified with ruin, works for Tom as Percy ends the novel in a one-sentence summation of this triumphant comedy: "To bed we go for a long winter's nap, twined about each other as the ivy twineth, not under a bush or in a car or on the floor or any such humbug as marked the past peculiar years of Christendom, but at home in bed where all good folks belong."

The epilogue is a triumph, the kind of gold we rarely find these days in fiction, and it is earned. It is difficult to think of any novel that ends on a note of such authentic affirmation. My own feeling about the novel can best be compared to the moment following the midnight mass where the children of some love couples and young Thomas More shoot off firecrackers. "Hurrah for Jesus Christ!" they cry, in another echo of Dostoevski. "Hurrah for the United States!"

Hurrah for Walker Percy! Hurrah for what is left of the USA! Maybe the New Eden did not work. On the other hand, given the peculiarity of the age, maybe there is yet time for every man to be a king, if only of a poor collard patch in the garden of being.

CLEANTH BROOKS

Walker Percy and Modern Gnosticism

It is dangerous to impute to one man ideas that belong to another, and as one reads the pages that follow, this may seem to be precisely the course that I am pursuing. But that is not at all my intention. I am not aware that Walker Percy has ever mentioned Gnosticism in any of his writings. Nor is it necessary, for what I have to say, that he should have done so. After all, why should any modern writer mention an ancient heresy of the first centuries of the Christian era?

Gnosticism, however, is far from dead. There is plenty of hard evidence that it pervades Western civilization. Consequently, the study of it, far from being a subject of merely antiquarian interest, could be indispensable for an understanding of the great intellectual movements that have convulsed our own century. Such at least is the contention of Eric Voegelin, whose monumental five-volume book, *Order and History,* is being published by the Louisiana State University Press. If Percy never mentions Gnosticism, neither has he, so far as I know, ever mentioned Voegelin and may never have read him. But again, that possibility does not figure in my present design which amounts to no more than pointing out some highly interesting and, I think, significant parallels between the writings of these two men. Yet if the parallelisms are genuinely significant, the readers of either Percy or Voegelin may benefit from the widened perspective effected by broadening for them the cultural context of each writer's work.

From *The Southern Review* 13, no. 4 (October 1977). © 1977 by Louisiana State University.

The basic resemblance between Percy and Voegelin that first struck me was the fact that both writers see modern man as impoverished by his distorted and disordered view of reality. As for Percy, I noticed it first in his novels. There, since he is a genuine novelist, the view is simply implied. It is, of course, spelled out in the essays that make up *The Message in the Bottle*. A comparable account of man's distorted perspective and an account of how it developed is the very theme and subject matter of all of Voegelin's writings for the last thirty years.

In all of Percy's novels the hero inherits what amounts to an orthodox Christian view of man and his relation to reality, but the world inhabited by the hero is dominated by ideas that are powerfully twisted away from any orthodox view. In the first three novels the heroes finally achieve, despite the age they live in, a religious apprehension of their own stance in the world. In the fourth novel, however, the protagonist is maddened by what he sees as the ineffectuality of Christianity in a world he finds intolerable. Vowing to take matters into his own hands, Lancelot becomes a modern Gnostic.

As I have remarked, the essays collected in *The Message in the Bottle* spell out Percy's estimate of the situation in which modern man finds himself. In the very first essay, Percy argues that a "theory of man must account for the alienation of man," but points out that the dominant ideas of the twentieth century do not and cannot. That is because they define alienation as a phenomenon located in this time and place, rather than recognize it as the necessary condition of man. But the anthropology of Judeo-Christianity has always seen alienation as man's essential condition. That tradition accounts for alienation through the doctrine of the Fall. According to this doctrine there occurred at the beginning of human history a separation or alienation of man from God, an alienation that accounted for, as Percy sees it, the "homelessness of man who (in this world) is not in fact at home." Moreover, the Judeo-Christian scheme provided, in its own terms, ways and means for man's becoming reconciled with God; but it did not promise him any heaven on this earth. The bliss of perfection and peace was to be recovered elsewhere, in eternity, and not in the world of time.

By contrast, the modern view regards man as only "a higher organism satisfying this or that need from its environment." Man thus can be made happy by a more perfect adjustment to his environment. Through the efforts of our marvelous technology, man can now hope to make radical modification of his environment and so perfect his adjustment to it.

Our scientists and humanists, therefore, have erased the notion of the Fall and have promised to take Man back to Eden; that is, to the perfect environment from which the Judeo-Christian account claimed that he had been expelled. But the new Eden will be real, no mere fable. It will be a place—as Percy rather sardonically puts it—"where scientists know like angels, and laymen prosper in good environments, and ethical democracies progress through education."

Unfortunately, however, this promised utopian Eden remains unrealized. Man remains alienated. As Percy explains in "The Delta Factor,"

> The scientists were saying that by science man was learning more and more about himself as an organism and more and more about the world as an environment and that accordingly the environment could be changed and man made to feel more and more at home.
>
> The humanists were saying that through education and the application of the ethical principles of Christianity, man's lot was certain to improve.
>
> But poets and artists and novelists were saying something else: that at a time when, according to the theory of the age, men should feel most at home they felt most homeless.
>
> Something was wrong.

Percy's view is that on this issue our poets and artists and novelists have been dead right. On earlier pages of this essay he asks a number of searching questions:

> Why has man entered on an orgy of war, murder, torture, and self-destruction unparalleled in history and in the very century when he had hoped to see the dawn of universal peace and brotherhood? . . .
>
> Why have more people been killed in the twentieth century than in all other centuries put together? . . .
>
> Why do young people look so sad, the very young who, seeing how sad their elders are, have sought a new life of joy and freedom with each other and in the green fields and forests, but who instead of finding joy look even sadder than their elders?

Percy has his own way of answering these questions. His readers will already know, or by further reading of his work, can learn, what his answers are. What I want to do here is to turn to Voegelin's description of the way in which modern man conceives of himself.

Like Percy, Voegelin interprets the various powerful drives of the modern age as heading up in a belief that utopia can be achieved. A perfect society of one sort or another is the goal, according to Voegelin, of all the modern manifestations of Gnosticism. But in this matter they inherit from the ancient Gnostics, who are their forebears in unbroken continuity. Like the modern scientists and humanists, the ancient Gnostic cults sought to erase the idea of any Fall of Man. They could not agree with what was proclaimed in *Genesis,* namely, that the Creation was essentially good—that it was the handiwork of a good God, who, in viewing his handiwork, had pronounced that "it was very good."

On the contrary, the ancient Gnostics held that the Creation was the work of a demon—a cruel demiurge. The world—with its mutability, sexuality, wickedness, and violence—is woefully imperfect, but man has the potentiality to be perfect if he does not confound himself with this imperfect world. Man had the misfortune to be placed in this flawed world not by his own error but by an evil god. His task then is to extricate himself from this evil world, partially at least by throwing off the bonds of his own evil flesh. Then he can get back, in spite of the obstructions set up by the demiurge, to the true god and achieve the more perfect order for which he was originally designed.

Two crucial aspects of Gnosticism are worth emphasizing here: (1) Man the creature is not responsible for the evil in which he finds himself. He has a right to blame it on someone or something else. The assumption that "In Adam's fall / We sinned all" is to the Gnostic pure nonsense. And (2) Man's salvation depends upon his own efforts. He must rely not upon faith but on gnosis, the secret knowledge that makes it possible for him to evade the snares and entanglements of the demon and to reunite his soul with the divinity from which he has come.

These two traits, Voegelin points out, continue to characterize Gnosticism, even in its present-day secularized form. Dissatisfied with the nature of reality, man can now the more confidently hope that, with his increasing knowledge, he can remake the world to suit himself. As Voegelin puts it, what is common to the profusion of "gnostic experiences and symbolic expression" is "the experience of the world as an alien place into which man has strayed and from which he must find his way back home to the other world of his origin." The divine spark within him is "an alien in this world and the world is alien to it."

The continuity of Gnosticism from the ancient Gnostic sects of the classical world on down to modern manifestations of this kind of speculation was worked out as early as the first half of the nineteenth century, largely by German and French scholars. That history is highly interesting, but it can have no part in this abbreviated essay. More to my purpose here are the

names of some of the modern thinkers whom Voegelin regards as Gnostics
and their different formulas for eliminating modern man's sense of alienation.

It will be interesting, for example, to compare with Voegelin's view what
Percy has to say about Karl Marx. Man has always been alienated, Percy
writes: "By the very cogent anthropology of Judeo-Christianity . . . human
existence was by no means to be understood as the transaction of a higher
organism satisfying this or that need from its environment, [either] by being
'creative' or enjoying 'meaningful relationships.' . . ." Rather, human existence was to be understood "as the journey of a wayfarer along life's way."
Not so for Marx. For him, as Percy puts it, "the experience of alienation
was . . . an inevitable consequence of capitalism." So Marx hoped to get rid
of capitalism, and expected that man's alienation would subsequently dis-
appear; without capitalism, man could be beautifully adapted to his environment and reconciled with himself.

According to Voegelin, "Marx is a speculative gnostic." Marx has convinced himself that he has penetrated the secret of history and therefore
knows the way in which it must go. The perfect society of the classless state
will be achieved through "the revolution of the proletariat and the transformation of man into the communist superman." But, according to Voegelin,
like all Gnostic utopians, Marx misrepresents the nature of man and for his
own purposes deforms the nature of reality.

Or consider Georg Friedrich Hegel. Martin Luschei writes that Percy
once told him that "After twelve years of scientific education . . . he felt
rather like Kierkegaard when he finished reading Hegel: 'Hegel,' said Kierkegaard, 'explained everything under the sun except one small detail, what
it means to be a man living in the world who must die.'" Furthermore,
Luschei quotes, with reference to Percy's reaction against abstraction, Kierkegaard's statement that Hegelian idealism had abolished "individual man,"
for "every speculative philosopher" had confused "himself with humanity
at large." In short, as Percy puts it with an amplitude that will cover Marx,
Hegel, and many another philosopher, German philosophy had for a long
time suffered from an "old interior itch" which turns too heavily to abstraction and as a consequence lets "the world slip away."

Voegelin would add further names—not limited to the German philos-
ophers and thinkers who had let "the world" and reality itself "slip away."
In fact, he would define the "old interior itch" as Gnosticism itself. "All
gnostic movements," he writes, "are involved in the project of abolishing the
constitution of being, with its origin in divine, transcendent being, and re-
placing it with a world-immanent order of being, the perfection of which

lies in the realm of human action." But specifically, what does Voegelin say about Hegel? For him, Hegel is another of the moderns who have, by willfully ignoring certain elements of humanity, promulgated a deformed conception of reality. Voegelin says, among other things, that the "factor [that] Hegel excludes [from reality] is the mystery of a history that wends its way into the future without knowing its end. History as a whole is essentially not an object of cognition; the meaning of the whole is not discernible." Nevertheless, Hegel's interior itch set him to constructing a history of man that was "fully comprehensible."

One could go on with Voegelin's roll call of other great Gnostics of later times—Hobbes, Comte, Nietzsche, Freud, Heidegger, et al. But I am here not writing an essay so much as setting down notes for an essay to be written. I shall limit myself therefore to only one more example, one that is the more interesting because it is highly problematic.

Saint Thomas More wrote a Utopia—indeed, coined the word. Does Voegelin regard him as a Gnostic? Well, no; but his treatment of More is very interesting.

> In his *Utopia* [Voegelin writes] More traces the image of man and of society that he considers perfect. To this perfection belongs the abolition of private property. Because he had the benefit of an excellent theological education, however, More is well aware that this perfect state cannot be achieved in the world: man's lust for possessions is deeply rooted in original sin, in *superbia* in the Augustinian sense. In the final part of his work when More looks over his finished picture, he has to admit that it would all be possible if only there were not the "serpent of superbia." But there *is* the serpent of superbia—and More would not think of denying it.

Is the protagonist of *Love in the Ruins,* Dr. Thomas More, a descendant of the Saint—is he a Gnostic? Well hardly, but Percy has been very careful not to make him a saint and, even more important, not to make him merely the embodiment of an abstract idea, even of an idea to which Percy is himself devoted.

Dr. Thomas More is a Roman Catholic, but Percy does not present him as a model of Christian piety. More enjoys bourbon whiskey—Early Times is clearly his favorite brand—and he is strongly attracted to a pretty girl—almost any pretty girl. He admits that he is a "bad Catholic." He says that he is like the Saint's second wife, a woman "who believed in God but saw no reason why one should disturb one's life [for Him], certainly not lose one's head."

In his novel, Percy has made the issue more complicated still—and thereby rendered his protagonist more thoroughly human—by having him invent the lapsometer, an instrument for making miraculous diagnoses of the human psyche, with the promise of reshaping humanity and, with it, the world. When More says, near the end of the novel, "I still believe my lapsometer can save the world," he sounds rather like a Gnostic himself. But the saving clause that follows—"if I can get it right"—and, still more, the sentence that follows in which he tells what he considers is wrong with the world, together indicate that he is no utopian. He has no ambition to create a new Adam. Apparently his modest ambition is to help with a highly necessary repair job on the old Adam, who now suffers from "chronic angelism-bestialism that rives soul from body and sets it orbiting the great world as the spirit of abstraction whence it takes the form of beasts, swans and bulls, werewolves, blood-suckers, Mr. Hydes, or just poor lonesome ghost locked in its own machinery." (René Descartes, thou shouldst be living at this hour—to witness where your classic riving of soul from body has left the modern world.)

Dr. More's vocation is that of a healer—so is Dr. Percy's—which is one way of saying that both are in the human repair business and that neither is a quietist or a defeatist, waiting for the civilization to collapse. But then, of course, neither is Eric Voegelin. There is a difference between (1) trying to put back together a world that is "broken, sundered, busted down," and (2) junking the world in favor of a fool-proof model that you have thought up in your own head.

All right, all right, the skeptical reader may say, but is there any positive justification for raising in Dr. Thomas More's case the complicated issue of Gnosticism? I think so, and the best way to show it is to listen to More's talk. He may be a "bad Catholic"—he may, for example, have let eleven years elapse before coming again to his father-confessor—but his theological orthodoxy is genuine, and he is himself quite conscious that it constitutes his anchor against the undertow of the powerful currents of modernity. What do we hear him saying—and what are some of the things said to him?

More says of the connection between revolution and totalitarianism: "Students are a shaky dogmatic lot. And the 'freer' they are, the more dogmatic. At heart they're totalitarians: they want either total dogmatic freedom or total dogmatic unfreedom, and the one thing that makes them unhappy is something in between." (Voegelin's "metaxy" is the "in-between state"—

between the animal and the divine, between the immanent and the transcendent—which is the peculiarly human realm.)

More, speaking of his first wife, remarks that "What she didn't understand, she being spiritual and seeing religion as spirit, was that it took religion to save me from the spirit world, from orbiting the earth like Lucifer and the angels, that it took nothing less than touching the thread off the misty interstates [Voegelin's metaxy again] and eating Christ himself to make me mortal man again and let me inhabit my own flesh and love her in the morning."

More is addressed by a revolutionist as follows: "Let me put it this way, Doctor. You know what we're going to do. We're going to build a new society right here." This statement has what Voegelin would call the genuine Gnostic ring: the speaker's absolute confidence that he knows the true state of affairs, an equal certainty about the soundness of his motives, and a genuine relishing of his sense of power.

The same accent is to be heard in what a revolutionary professor says to More, though his speech also exhibits the not uncommon Gnostic ruthlessness. The professor is voicing his praise of a certain (mythical) Latin-American dictator. He says: "He's the George Washington of Ecuador, the only man beloved north and south and the only man capable of uniting the country." When More asks whether he "didn't kill several hundred thousand Ecuadorians who didn't love him," the professor is at no loss for a reply: "Yes, but they were either fascists or running dogs or lackeys of the American imperialists. Anyhow, the question has become academic."

In this general connection, it will be interesting to cite More on the subject of what he calls "angelism," which, as I interpret it, arises from the human being's impatience with the limitations of the mortal mind—impatience with perceptions mediated through the senses, the progress of thought from the known to the unknown, and dependence upon common sense and reason. A man who has fallen into "angelism," Dr. More tells us, "will fall prey to the first abstract notion proposed to him and will kill anybody who gets in his way, torture, execute, wipe out entire populations, all with the best possible motives and the best possible intentions, in fact in the name of peace and freedom, etcetera." Angelism, then, is essentially Gnostic and potentially violent. Thus Voegelin's account of twentieth-century Gnosticism in action includes, along with those of milder Gnostics, the names of very violent ones like Stalin and Hitler. The point is that a Gnostic impatience with human limitations can easily convert into a hubristic denial of one's own limitations and an amoral disregard for ethical systems demanding decency in the human community.

That seems to be what happens to Lancelot Andrewes Lamar, the character whom Walker Percy has presented as the complete twentieth-century Gnostic—a millenialist through and through—confident that he knows how to reform a corrupt world and willing to kill if he cannot cure. In Percy's latest novel, *Lancelot,* the protagonist says of his own quest: "So Sir Lancelot set out, looking for something rarer than the Grail. A sin." But Lance discovers only "buggery," not sin. (Of course, he fails to look within himself.) His basic assumption is that "Original Sin is not something man did to God but something God did to man. . . ." In other words, Lance, like an ancient Gnostic, would blame God—or a cruel demiurge—for the world's imperfections, rather than take any of the blame upon himself.

Lance sees his task as dissociation from and purification of this evil world. He decides: "I cannot tolerate this age. What is more, I won't. That [when he destroyed Belle Isle and four people on it] was my discovery: that I didn't have to." Instead, "there is going to be a new order of things and I shall be part of it." He will begin a "new Reformation," a "Third Revolution" in America, the first having been "won at Yorktown," the second "lost at Appomattox." Lance then believes both principal tenets of Gnosticism—that man is not responsible for evil and that his salvation depends on his own efforts.

At several points in *Lancelot,* Percy juxtaposes Lance's answers with Christianity's. Lance himself explains his extremism in terms of the church's apparent defection: "I cannot tolerate this age. And I will not. I might have tolerated you and your Catholic Church, and even joined it, if you had remained true to yourself. Now you're part of the age." The church, in Lance's Gnostic vision, has confounded itself by being a part of this world. In the book's ending, Lancelot and his friend Percival, a Roman Catholic priest, agree, not on that issue but on the absoluteness of their own alternative visions: Lancelot says, "One of us is wrong. It will be your way or it will be my way." And the priest answers "*Yes.*"

The ending of *Lancelot* is ambiguous, but I think that Percy juxtaposes the speaker and the auditor, the Gnostic and the Christian, in order to suggest that we are indeed in an either/or situation. *Either* we accept alienation as our necessary condition—acknowledging the world's evil condition and helping to ameliorate it, but never presuming to believe that we can eliminate it—and live in faith, *or* we will find our own theories inviting and condoning the Hitlers, the Idi Amins, and the Lancelots of the world.

For many readers, the millenialism of Lancelot Lamar will be obscured by the fact that his condemnation of the modern world may easily appear to be Walker Percy's own. This well may be. Many who share Percy's values also share Lancelot's belief that we are living in Sodom. The priest Percival evidently concurs with Lancelot about the corruption of the modern world. But one can agree with Lance that the world is corrupt without agreeing at all with his single-minded resolution: "I will start a new world single-handedly or with those like me who will not tolerate [the present world]. . . . We know what we want. And we'll have it. If it takes the sword, we'll use the sword." He is completely prepared to get rid of the world itself, for he is confident that he can devise a better one. Percival, however, is not so presumptuous nor so self-righteous—and neither, for that matter is Walker Percy.

There is hardly need to go on. Clearly Percy and Voegelin are more than superficially alike in their diagnosis of the present state of the culture. Modern man has a disordered notion of what he is and therefore a deformed conception of reality. For a succinct account of the modern situation and how it developed, one might well look at the Introduction to Voegelin's *Science, Politics, and Gnosticism.* But I am not using this essay to ask Percy to adopt Voegelin's terms or to suggest to Voegelin that in his studies of modernity he give more attention to some of the special problems so brilliantly dramatized in Percy's novels. Indeed, I would consider it presumptuous to offer counsel to either man. My more modest intention is to suggest to Walker Percy's readers that the basic themes of Percy's novels are not merely the private and special insights of an important novelist, and are certainly not to be regarded as the privileged crankiness of a somewhat eccentric Roman Catholic intellectual. They have a close relation to a powerful and searching criticism of the modern world, of which Voegelin is clearly the major exemplar, but which in the last decade has begun to claim the attention and the endorsement of an increasing number of modern scholars.

JOYCE CAROL OATES

Lancelot

Walker Percy is one of our most engaging stylists, an original and rather quirky "Southern" novelist who resists facile classifications. He is the author of two excellent novels—*The Moviegoer* and *The Last Gentleman*—and an ambitious though flawed satirical novel, *Love in the Ruins: The Adventures of a Bad Catholic at a Time Near the End of the World.* Not long ago he published a sequence of essays on language, *The Message in the Bottle,* which a linguist friend of mine assures me is fiction also; but there is much in it to admire, and a great deal to provoke thought. And it is beautifully written.

Percy has acquired the reputation of being a "philosophical thinker," which seems to have meant that he has had ideas about such weighty people as Kierkegaard, Heidegger, Sartre and Camus; but I have never really found in his fiction much evidence to support this view, and no evidence at all that he has responded in an unusually deep or subtle or original way to the complex world-views elaborated by these men. From the very first, in Percy's evocation of New Orleans and his portrayal of Binx the Moviegoer, a man dying slowly of boredom, he has been wonderfully alive to the sounds and textures and odors of life, and his ability to render the baffling solidity of the world made his prose sing with vitality. In *The Moviegoer* and *The Last Gentleman* Percy re-created familiar worlds for us and populated them with odd, rather marvelous characters, sometimes tending toward caricature but memorable nonetheless. No genuine writer of fiction need rely upon philo-

From *The New Republic* 176, no. 6 (February 5, 1977). © 1977 by *The New Republic, Inc.*

sophical "ideas"—and it was hardly abstract notions of freedom, determinism, existential *angst,* alienation, etc. that made these novels so irresistible. They were artistically and humanly rich, and beautifully crafted.

Love in the Ruins, however, was a self-indulgent and rather shrill venture, an attempt on Percy's part to project into the 1980s certain of the social, racial and religious issues of the '60s. *Lancelot* continues this satiric tone, consisting for the most part of a lengthy and crotchety denunciation of what Percy sees to be the sickness of contemporary society. Though there is a story of sorts fleshed out about Lancelot's manic discontent with the world, the other characters are curiously flat and vaporous, hardly more than assemblages of shrewdly noted details, and one is left in the company of a confused and embittered man of the sort who might spend his days writing incoherent letters to the editors of local newspapers:

> California? The West? That's where the two intersect: Billy Graham, Richard Nixon, Las Vegas, drugs, pornography, and every abstract discarnate idea ever hit upon by man roaming the wilderness in search of habitation.

> Washington, the country, is down the drain. Everyone knows it. The people have lost it to the politicians, bureaucrats, drunk Congressmen, lying Presidents, White House preachers, C.I.A., F.B.I., Mafia, Pentagon, pornographers, muggers, buggers, bribers, bribe takers, rich crooked cowboys, sclerotic Southerners, rich crooked Yankees, dirty books, dirty movies, dirty talk shows, dirty soap operas, fags, lesbians, abortionists . . . dying cities, dying schools. . . .

It does not matter much that Lancelot, the self-conscious "scion of an old family," is meant to be an ambiguous character, part madman, part sage, an Old Testament prophet screeching against the sins of others while befuddled by (and intoxicated with) his own; nor does it matter that his first-person confession is narrated to a faceless, invisible priest, in what is evidently a mental hospital. His simple-minded prejudices and quixotic dreams for the future are uncomfortably close to ideas Percy has expressed elsewhere, with less vehemence and more art. Though the plot of *Lancelot* is a tired and contrived one involving a cuckolded husband's revenge upon his wife and her decadent friends (for whom we feel, perversely, far more sympathy than we feel for the garrulous and self-righteous central character), it is nevertheless preferable to the empty rhetoric that fills page after page of the novel. Percy is evidently disgusted with what he imagines to be the contemporary world, where "fags" and "lesbians" and "whores" are much in evidence, and where a gentleman experiences difficulty in distinguishing a "lady" from a "whore." Lancelot returns often to this peculiar problem and envisions a kind of Disneyland paradise where all uncomfortable ambiguities are erased:

> We know who we are and where we stand. There will be leaders and there will be followers. . . . There will be men who are strong and pure of heart. . . . There will be virtuous women who are proud of their virtue and there will be women of the street . . . and everyone will know which is which. You can't tell a whore from a lady now, but you will then.

> Freedom? The New Woman will have perfect freedom. She will be free to be a lady or a whore.

If Percy only takes his hero halfway seriously, presenting his desperately "evil" gesture as a sort of Dostoyevskian plunge into suffering (Lancelot murders several people, not very convincingly), it is still the case that such nonsense is nonsense on the page and grievously weakens his novel. Again and again Lancelot returns to the "problem" of female liberation, the "problem" of needing to divide women into ladies and whores and of dealing with them appropriately. When his simple-minded but vivacious young wife loses interest in him and takes on both an acting career and a lover, and plans on travelling to London to make a film, Lancelot deliberately plans her murder, and though he complains of a certain "coldness" and "numbness" of the spirit at the novel's conclusion, it isn't altogether clear that the author considers him mad. Misguided, perhaps, but fundamentally justified. We live in Sodom, don't we?—where "voracious" women have the power to turn hapless young men into homosexuals? (Lancelot's son has become a "mild" homosexual as a result of the appetites of overly-liberated young girls.) Therefore it's a worthwhile endeavor, the seeking of the unholy grail of evil. The faceless Catholic priest (with his painfully symbolic name Percival/Parsifal) seems to be offering Lancelot absolution at the end of the novel, for he assures him that there is a "new life" awaiting him once he leaves the mental hospital.

There are, of course, many fine, winning passages in *Lancelot*, especially in the opening chapters when the mad hero is more lyric than bitter. Though we hear Binx behind Lancelot's voice much of the time, his perceptions are comically dry and convincing, and when Percy's style is good it carries all before it:

> The mystery lies in the here and the now. The mystery is: What

is one to do with oneself? As you get older you realize the trick time is playing, and that unless you do something about it, the passage of time is nothing but the encroachment of the horrible banality of the past on the pure future. The past devours the future like a tape recorder, converting pure possibility into banality. . . .

There are light, deft comic characterizations of actors, one of them a very handsome young leading man named Dana who is a complete cipher, and whom directors adore because they "can create him from the beginning like a doll." Dana is so stupid he barely had sense not to drown when he fell off his surfboard in *Beach Blanket Bingo*. In the trashy movie being filmed at Lancelot's mansion he represents the life-force and is, in the glib words of one of the moviemakers, "The new Christ, of course." Percy is always good at creating a certain kind of part-liberated black, and his characterization of a restless millionaire Texan as a shrewd moron is a comic one. It's difficult to know, however, whether these people are to be taken seriously, or whether Percy means them to be stereotypes.

If there is a central problem with *Lancelot,* it is this confusion of tones, this mixture of genres. The novel seems incompletely realized in a number of ways. Throughout, Lancelot is addressing his old friend Percival, who has come to visit him in the hospital, but Percival is never allowed into the story— neither the present story, nor the past; he does not figure in the narrative at all. Yet one has the feeling that Percy must have originally intended to bring him into Lancelot's life in a meaningful way. There are other nagging inconsistencies. We are told repeatedly that Lancelot's and Margot's early married life was very happy, and we are treated rather more than is necessary to detailed descriptions of the pair's antic love-making (which for some reason are flatly unconvincing: Percy is a master at delineating ennui but shrill and over-wrought when it comes to passion), yet we are also told that the couple often drank themselves into oblivion and that Lancelot had become, over the years, near-catatonic in a state of constant alcoholic stupor. How is it possible that a healthy, happy marriage should involve such excessive drinking? Margot is described as fetchingly attractive at times, and at other times absurdly gross—as when she blows her nose with her fingers on Royal Street of New Orleans, or eats her breakfast "like a horse." Percy wishes to mock the woman and yet he must build her up, he must force us to believe in Lancelot's regard for her; otherwise Lancelot's desire for revenge will not seem believable. But the novel shows the strain and one soon ceases to care what happens to the characters, for it is evident that the author is merely manipulating them from scene to scene.

Lancelot himself is a familiar Percy character. He is alternately eloquent and garrulous; a failed lawyer, an idler, a television news addict as Binx was a movie addict—despite the fact that nothing ever happens on the television news. He speaks of evil, and of the Devil, and of sin, and of the disappointing direction the contemporary Catholic Church has taken, as if his very idleness and lack of involvement with the world gave him a certain authority. Meant to be Stavrogin, he sounds rather more like Marmeladov; and one cannot help but be offended by his continual smug superiority when he speaks of "women" and of "liberals." If for some people involvement in civil rights issues in the '60s was merely fashionable, a way of passing the time, it is hardly the case that all liberals shared Lancelot's—or is it Percy's?—bemused detachment.

If *Lancelot* is one of the most disappointing novels I have read in recent years, it is perhaps a tribute to the promise that Percy's earlier works have made; and I have no doubt that he will write richer and far more convincing novels in the future.

RICHARD PINDELL

Toward Home: Place, Language, and Death in The Last Gentleman

In a scene in Hawthorne's *The Blithedale Romance* the novel's excessively romantic hero, Miles Coverdale, stands meditatively before a window when a dove flies directly toward him, swerves, and then vanishes, as does also "the slight, fantastic pathos with which he had invested her." Coverdale readily invests the dove with portent because, after millennia of symbolic associations, both he and Hawthorne's reader agree on the dove's specialness. A dove flies on extended wings in whatever stately mansions of the soul. But now suppose, the postmodern reader is tempted to ask, we were to change before Coverdale's very eyes that dove into a pigeon. The embarrassing predicament that would ensue finds its artist in Walker Percy.

Entropy (the pigeon) and news (the dove) are the generating poles of *The Last Gentleman*. The novel dramatizes a contest for the attention of Will Barrett, the title character; he is torn between a stagnant mentality of entropy and an imaginative expectancy of news. Two rival arts of being here, one essentially entropic or reductive, the other essentially news-making or creative, converge on the prime world-making *materia* of place, language, and death. Out of these three phenomena Percy bodies forth Will's inwardness and tracks his possibilities, and failures, of progress toward receptivity to news. Finally it is within an imagination of home that Percy advances and unifies the dialectic relationships within place, language, and death. By so doing, he seeks to restate man in such a way as to possess him of his potential.

From *The Art of Walker Percy: Stratagems for Being.* © 1979 by Louisiana State University Press.

I shall center this essay in a discussion mainly of three emblematic scenes which exemplify the workings of the imagination of home: Will and Kitty's failed love-making in the Central Park "sniper's den"; Will's visit to Valentine Vaught's piney-woods mission school; and Will's attendance at the deathbed baptism of Jamie Vaught.

Percy begins Will's journey in Central Park at "ground zero." The term is well calculated to record the terrifically emptying impact of a historical climax, when the dove of epiphany turns into the pigeon of entropy. The climate of loss is total. Entropy defines itself here as the measure of disorder consequent to postmodern leveling. "Nothing is *really* real for mankind," says a commentator on Romano Guardini's *The End of the Modern World,* "until it can be located, until man can find it in some given place." The statement is an apt journey text for Will, who is, perhaps, the most explicitly place-conscious character in Western literature. But in the detritus of vanished landmarks and forgotten unities at ground zero, how can anybody or anything be located and thereby realized?

Such a crisis of orientation informs Will's occupation with Kitty one night in a rocky hideaway in Central Park: "The place was down a ravine choked with dogbane and whortleberry and over a tumble of rocks into a tiny amphitheater, a covert so densely shaded that its floor was as bare as cave's dirt. By day it looked very like the sniper's den on Little Round Top which Mathew Brady photographed six weeks after the battle: the sniper was still there! a skeleton in butternut, his rifle propped peaceably against the rocks." The redundancy of place-notation—"amphitheater," "covert," "cave," "den"—is neither idle nor mistaken. In this parcel of delocalized acreage Will, whose chronic amnesia symbolizes among other things contemporary self-absence, needs to memorize where he is! The accumulating rhetoric of dwelling resounds his effort to persuade himself he is a somebody somewhere rather than a nobody nowhere. In the end he only feigns inhabitation. The impossible transmigration of locale through Brady's camera and Will's memory dramatically exposes Will's substituting a preoccupation with place for any real occupation of space.

Significantly, in the sentence immediately following the above description of the place, Will seems to take his cue from the dead sniper. Preparing to embrace Kitty, he acts out the sniper's relinquishment of his rifle: "He set the police special in the dust beside him." At this point in Will's journey the sniper is his ironic occupational model. Like a sniper, Will stands outside the space, both inner and outer, that he is meant to control or, at the very least, contest. Unoccupied by himself and well-nigh, like Central Park itself, a public space, he is up for claim by whatever aggressive local, past, or fantasy presence. (The same holds true for Kitty. While Will orients himself toward a historic impossibly transplanted spirit of place, Kitty is a mouthpiece of the *Zeitgeist,* whose leveling presence solicits from her the forms of behavior preached by its myriad quack ontologists and faddish lifestylists.) At ground zero Will is the nothingness though which we see, as through a ghost, the landscape.

The *sniper* is one of a cluster of space-control designations—*janitor, engineer, proprietor, Adam, genius loci*—which throughout Will's journey function in a choric role, vis-à-vis his sources and methods of self-orientation. The repetition of these designations suggests Will's desperate but unfulfilled need to place himself. The term *proprietor,* as Will is sometimes called in reference to his ownership of the two-hundred-acre remnant of the old family plantation in Mississippi, is particularly summational, as is *planter,* a variant form of *proprietor.* Will is "the strangest of planters, proprietor of two hundred acres of blackberries and canebrakes," and Percy puns on Will's strenuous efforts to "plant" himself in the root-resistant debris of leveled landscapes. Taken socially, *proprietor* betokens Will's last gentlemanship—his honorable upholding of old-fashioned proprieties. As such, *proprietor* achieves succinct biographical descriptiveness: Will is character in search of personality. Turning its traditional connotation of territorial suzerainty completely inward, *proprietor* at once comments ironically on Will's vacancy—he is both literally and psychospatially an absentee landlord—and underlines the necessity of self-sovereignty incumbent upon him.

One cannot be a proprietor without language; for to name something is to claim sovereignty over it and to be unable to name it is to fail to establish sovereignty. Farther along in his journey, during his brief visit to Valentine Vaught's pineywoods mission school in Alabama, Will learns as much. For it is at Val's that language is introduced as the peculiarly human mode of sovereignty over inner and outer space. With Val in south Alabama, he sees how, as existential model, *proprietor* intersects with and yields to *Adam,* who was first landlord of the creatures in the Garden because he was their namer.

Val's mission settlement in the pines is likened to a "place of crude and makeshift beginnings on some blasted planet." This landscape, a vision of the world after the Bomb, logically succeeding ground zero, stages a confrontation between the word and pure space, which asserts language's first and immemorial task: the provision of an order within and a shelter from space. Scene and event at Val's, conversation and underconversation, all espouse the spatio-temporal lordship of language. Language is presented in its highest power: naming. "When they do suddenly break into the world of language," Val tells Will of her backward pupils, "it is something to see. They are like Adam on the First Day. What's that? they ask me. That's a hawk, I tell them and they believe me. . . . They were not alive and then they are and so they'll believe you." Naming particularizes language's power of placement. A name gives the named thing "form and habitation," that is, a negotiable shape and a conjured setting, wherein it is let free to declare itself. Through naming the namer gains admittance to the going agreements about what is real that we call the truth, and the world begins to assume for him the recognizable features of a place. Naming confers reality not only on the thing named but on the namer; it is both a giving and a receiving of news. Naming is the Eureka bond between a person and the other: that which was lost is found.

As a mode of placement, naming is not only a celebrative act, one, that is, which occasions a reciprocal greeting between namer and named, but a competitive act as well. By his words man competes with the given for room to live. Through language he endeavors to wrest himself free from what around him conduces to inertia. This rivalry between language and thingness, the verbal and the reific, is dramatized early in the novel in a flashback to the summer when Will worked in his father's law firm. There he would overhear his father "speak with his clients, a murmurous sound compounded of grievance and redress. As the summer wore on, it became more and more difficult to distinguish the words from the sound, until finally they merged with the quarrels of the sparrows under the windowsill and the towering sound of the cicadas that swelled up from the vacant lots and filled the white sky." The surrounding space breaks down the words spoken in it, converting them into its own mindless din, an ironic Babel of "towering sound." Language is naturalized, leaving Will ludicrously adream and speechless among the beasts, tending his allergy-swollen "great baboon's nose." The tone is light enough. But behind the mocking squib of Darwin upside down is a monitory truth: the leveling of language—the disintegration of news into noise—risks the loss of man.

Because of the crucially sensitive political relationship between language and space, Barrett could not establish sovereignty in the "sniper's den" scene. The trial-and-error naming of the Central Park hideaway—"amphitheater," "covert," "cave" and finally "sniper's den," as it is thereafter designated— is in its very tentativeness and redundancy a travesty of the Adamic function. Language serves a mnemonic rather than a nominative purpose. The name settled upon, in that it is borrowed from another time and place, approaches the height of namelessness—interchangeability. (For a name, like a place, is a concentration of energy, felt as a presence, within *inimitable* bounds.) Unnamed, the place arrogates to itself decisive powers. "Setting" overturns its meaning, moving from complement to whole, stage to stage-manager. The place not only lends Will and Kitty a separate audience, but also, one senses, dictates what they say. Kitty, for whom the hideaway acts as a test space for her sexually liberated consciousness, speaks of her love for the dance; Will, for whom the place acts as a sensorium for his nostalgic and topophiliac fantasies, speaks of an ancestor who fell at the siege of Petersburg. But concomitant with the weakening of language's spatial authority has come a decline in its exchange value. Neither party hears the other. Speech degenerates into speeches, dialogue into monologue. In the darkness they have difficulty "placing" each other even by touch. Will fully clothed, Kitty naked, they lie beside each other full of words and incommunicado. Their failed love-making is appropriate because their language carries no spatio-temporal lordship. Unable to possess the place, they are unable to possess themselves or each other. Utterance is reduced to a form of existential absence. Despoiled of their sovereignty, the two remain vacancies in a void.

As a paradigm of postmodern man's increasing inability to take place, the "sniper's den" scene includes as well the two principal shapers of the entropic landscape: history and science. Under the aegis of these two forces, which converge in Brady's camera, Will and Kitty perform their emptiness. Will labors under the burden of historical superfluousness. With the major exception of Val's place, most of the places in his journey, until he reaches the desert, are already occupied by the dead. The environs of a Bear Mountain ski lodge are dominated by a "shadowy knoll associated by tradition with Mad Anthony Wayne," and the golf course adjacent to the Vaughts' in Alabama is "haunted by the goddess Juno and the spirit of the great Bobby Jones." In the "sniper's den" scene the dead sniper's solid reality and serene repose contrast markedly with Will's and Kitty's somewhat laborious compilation of evidence that they exist. An apt gloss on the scene is this reflection of Frederick Brown's: "Like Beckett's anti-heroes, we inhabit nowhere; only the dead, happily immured, enjoy place." Also like Beckett's antiheroes, we are upstaged by these unriddable corpses. Their stubborn vitality, their continuing displacement of our space—"the sniper was still there!"—consigns us to the ghostly realm of the vicarious. In places predominated by another presence one's gestures easily become histrionic, mimetic. (As we have noted, Will's putting down his police special involuntarily mimics the sniper's relinquishment of his rifle; the historically rich corpse momentarily serves Will as a stand-in self.) The "cave" of man's beginnings has become the "amphitheater" of the end game, in which the obscurely exhausted players pile parody upon parody, as if trying to sustain the illusion of having something to parody.

Where history preempts individual living space by the sheer redundancy of its overkept accumulations, science usurps it by its attractive methods of acquisition. "The price of the beauty and the elegance of the method of science = the dispossession of [the] layman." By ordaining the analytic faculty as the only credible, or sufficiently beautiful, locus of event, science disinherits its users of the world it opens to them. People are specialized out of existence. "It suited them [Will and Jamie] to lie abed, in the Trav-L-Aire yet also in old Carolina, listening to baseball in Cleveland and reading about set theory and an Englishman holed up in Somerset." Place, baffled through a trunk line of exotic transmissions, reduces to nonplace: Old Carolina, "a region immersed in place and time," to a site of "abstract activity which could take place anywhere else, a map coordinate." Characteristic of the false art of being-here, the law of change at work is not creative but cooptative. In this scene in the camper, results parody needs by substituting their opposites: mediation is taken over by media, participation by consumption. The place is, in effect, bracketed by history, presuming to be the record of the past, and by science, presuming to be the record of the future, but the occupants are not present. Indeed, the meticulous placing of the two travelers merely begs the question, where are they? Often such reality-loss, in an intolerable intensification of emptiness, can lead to panic. Periodically Will is beset by swarms of unlocalized fears called "ravenous particles." At such times he is desolately terrorized by a cessation of being without the release of death. But this scene, which so well demonstrates Max Frisch's shrewd observation, "technology . . . the knack of so arranging the world that we don't have to experience it," is as cozy as it is precisionistic. Plainly Will is lost in admiration for what separates him from experience.

If postmodern man remains enthralled in the idolatry of his own creations or, more precisely, in the *idolatry of his omissions,* can he hear news? In the deathbed baptism scene the dying Jamie Vaught, who has sent for a book on entropy, receives, instead, news of his salvation. But Will hears only words. "Here," says Percy of this scene, "Barrett has eliminated Christianity. That is gone. That is no longer even to be considered. . . . He *misses* it!" Will fails to make the discovery of his fundamental identity upon which the hearing of news depends. He misses what he is. "Man," says Percy, "is alienated by the nature of his being here. He is here as a stranger and as a pilgrim, which is the way alienation is conceived in my books." In *The Last Gentleman* alienation is rehabilitated from its emotional unrecognizability as a literary theme and established not as the agon of a particular age but as the universal human condition.

The second Fall of Man, then, is not to recognize his first one. Man perpetuates his forgetfulness of his fundamental identity as a pilgrim stranger—Will's amnesia is representative—by supposing himself an organism adapting to an environment. Postulating for himself the latter's pure ecological connectedness, he, in effect, dissembles his alienation and lives in bad faith. Will is scandalized in the deathbed baptism scene by the homely, makeshift performance of the rite and the overpowering stench of death. His aroused rote defense of his Episcopalian raising, in order to invoke right appearances and exempt him from the Catholic priest's proceedings, is but the ceremony of his innocence. Even as he involuntarily uses religion to evade religion, so his social embarrassment completely conceals his ontological embarrassment. For, as a pilgrim stranger, Will is born embarrassed, born at a loss.

Suppression of real human identity with a parody of it is the ironic point of another scene, which the deathbed baptism forcefully recalls. There in a New York hospital the occasion is Jamie's temporal rather than eternal birthday. By way of celebration, "the interns made a drink of laboratory alcohol and frozen grapefruit juice, as if they were all castaways and had to make do with what they had." With their peculiarly adaptive drink (in the hospital surroundings the "laboratory alcohol" crudely suggests sterilization and preservation) the celebrants secure themselves as organisms in an environment. Then in a prodigy of imposture they pretend to be what they are—"castaways"! The festivities take on the astonishing obliviousness, the self-perpetuating unreality, of the dancing on the *Titanic*.

Later Will's identity is presented to him, albeit unapprehended by him, in a parody of the Fall. Regaining consciousness, but not memory, on the camper seat after falling and striking his head on a monument during a campus uprising, Will asks, "'Oh, where is this place? . . . Where am I bound and what is my name?'" For all the novel's marvelously sensed catalogue of places, this nowhere (echoing God's question to Adam after the Fall, "Where art thou?") is *The Last Gentleman*'s symbolic center. For the three questions Will asks after his fall evoke, respectively, place, death and home, and language; thus they couch in the riddling manner of oracular utterances, clues to their answers. Man is a die-er and a home-goer, that is, a pilgrim stranger—a wanderer to a fixed and unknown point. He is also, it follows from his homelessness on this earth, a placer and a namer; the latter two corollary identities refer to his ways of taking charge of time and space. Man, in sum, is potentially a *sovereign* pilgrim stranger.

The sovereignty of man, the efficacy of his placing and naming, the most felicitous possible fulfillment of his being here, roots directly in his lived nomination of himself as a pilgrim stranger. Will misplaces himself because he misnames himself. In the "sniper's den" scene his self-locating gesture is an elaborate falsification of his fundamental identity. In a superimposition of the Gettysburg sniper's den he seeks to convert area into place by installing in the Central Park hideaway a place-presence—the aura of the dead sniper. But a place, we remember, is a concentration of energy, felt as a presence, within inimitable bounds. Like a name, a place is not interchangeable. Indeed, traditionally, a *genius loci* exists coterminous and consubstantial with its place in guarantee of that place's incalculable individuality and absolute immovability. Ostensibly a placer, Will here is really an antiplacer. He contributes to the pervasive leveling of place occurring today, when the sound of the bulldozer is heard even, and especially, in the place-rich South; there the novel's "loess" and "moraine"—soils transported from elsewhere—characterize a landscape accumulating toward the extinction of places. Will's promotion of delocalization in his apparent resistance to it exposes his in-trained environmental view of things. Ultimately the sniper, whom, as we have seen, he briefly mimicks, is established as the external stimulus that conditions his behavior. Overlooking his pilgrim strangerhood, Will construes himself as an organism adapting to an environment. Therefore he is hard put in the pitch darkness of the "sniper's den" literally to "place" Kitty or, symbolically, himself. Brady's camera symbolizes the encroaching invisibility of himself and his world. "People in the modern age," says Percy, "took photographs by the million: to prove despite their deepest suspicions to the contrary that they were not invisible."

Postmodern man's mistaken identity is both source and consequence of the contemporary denaturing of language. Will's failure of sovereignty, it is true, follows his misnaming of the "sniper's den" but such misnaming creates a condition in which naming can hardly be true. Instead, we have false naming—the naming that kills—when the name comes to obscure the thing. Such a fundamental slippage between names and their referents further vitiates language itself. We see how such a double-speaking process works in the language used by Lamar Thigpen. Contemplating with self-consciously heroic complacency the Vaughts' three black servants waving a picturesque farewell from the back steps, Lamar says, " 'There's nothing like the old-timey ways! . . .' even though the purple castle didn't look much like an antebellum mansion and the golf links even less like a cotton plantation." Despite the radical change of the picture its caption is read the same. Language is reduced to a parody of its nominative and presentational function.

Increasingly, phenomena drift about unnamed. The age itself, the frequent "nowadays" of the novel, lacks a name; "postmodern" is a stopgap no-name, which, like the expression, "the hereafter," admits only the expectation of chronological sequence and the complete ignorance of our fate. Detached from the things they are meant to articulate, words increasingly appear, in effect, in quotation marks. The word *intimate,* for example, is relegated to precisely this status as a possible adjective for Will and Kitty's contact without communication in the "sniper's den."

But identity and sovereignty can be positively interrelated; for man's discovery of his pilgrim strangerhood is the dislocation that makes things visible. With Will, journeying under the post-postlapsarian curse of mediateness, which divides him from his every activity, things are either so far away they are merely picturesque or so close they block themselves out. Minus a countering identity to focus things, Will is fixated or engulfed by them. But the recognition of the otherness of things and persons makes mediation possible, as opposed to mediateness; and with mediation, reciprocity; with reciprocity, love. When Jamie Vaught, confronted by his own death, in a sovereign act of self-choosing, in effect, christens himself a pilgrim stranger, he becomes, in Flannery O'Connor's phrase, "a realist of distances." That is why he hears news and Will only words.

Will's journey with terminally ill Jamie Vaught is also a death vigil, a postmodern installment on the theme of "as I lay dying." The deathbed baptism scene powerfully enacts the novel's major explicit premise, its working creative principle: "The certain availability of death is the very condition of recovering onself." Thus the intensification in the novel of the memento mori establishes as man's last hope his last extremity. Man is a die-er. Death is a going, a progress. *Homo moriens* is *homo viator.* Implicit in the recognition of the personal reality of death is the demand to be oneself—a pilgrim stranger, a placer, and a namer. For death, the distance between man and home, is the distance between man and the other. While false naming kills, true naming, then, gives life. "What's that? they ask me. That's a hawk, I tell them, and they believe me. . . . They were not alive and then they are and so they'll believe you." Hence Valentine Vaught, when in this way she presents language as naming and naming as news, is portrayed as a death figure: "a woman dressed in black, feeding entrails to a hawk in a chicken coop. She looked familiar. He eyed her, wondering whether he knew her." The faraway model here is Orpheus, who, presiding over the giving of life to things in the form of names, sojourned in the realms of both the dead and the living. The topic at Val's, in short, is incarnation. As Val hand-feeds the chicken hawk chicken "gut[s]," she refers to her bishop as "chicken-hearted"; and later Val, whose lovelessness keeps her more a symbol than a fulfillment of mediational and affective powers, admits to hating certain people's "guts." "Mind, in order to bear its witness," says Gide, "cannot do without matter. Hence the mystery of the incarnation." The wit of the primitive punning is wit-ness to that mystery. If the word is man's ever materializing, ever vanishing bond with things, death is the bond between the man-made word and the thing it names. It engenders the numen, the presence, that makes the name represent the thing. Death is the transfiguring factor. It is the defamiliarizing familiar, which brings things forth in their forgotten strangeness. As the deathbed baptism scene shows, the possibility of news depends upon the credibility of death.

But death has, like place and language, borne the brunt of postmodern leveling. It is suppressed by the new prudery which reduces death the ineffable to death the unspeakable. "Death is as outlawed now as sin used to be," remarks Sutter Vaught in his journal." Percy's task in the course of the novel is to resurrect the personal reality of death. To this end, in the deathbed baptism scene, as opposed to the "sniper's den" scene, not the dead but death itself is present. "There arose to the engineer's [Will's] nostrils first an intimation, like a new presence in the room, a somebody, then a foulness beyond the compass of smell." The fallen sniper is but one of a number of historic personages evoked in Will's journey that, together with historic events and scientific products and method, are deployed by Will to ornament his vacancy. There death is picturesque. Here death is grotesque. There death serves to lend Will a semblance, however false, of place. Here, working as the modern avatar of the sublime, which Thomas Mann accredits to the grotesque, death is essentially displacing. It becomes, in Heidegger's words, that "strange and unhomely thing that banishes us once and for all from everything in which we are at home." Astonishingly, in fact, death, the "presence," the "somebody," in the room, merges with the "*genius loci* of [the] Western desert," described as a "free-floating sense of geographical transcendence." Death and home, scene and change of scene, coexist in one unified potentiality. A stereotypical non-place—the hospital room—becomes in its numenization a place, and place itself is now finally defined as *anywhere one hears news of home.*

Here, squarely under the Δ sign, a kind of transvestiture occurs: the dying man puts on life, the living one puts on, unwittingly, death. Making placelessness radiant, death repeats the ontological imperative of ground zero: out of nothing Will must make something; he must fabricate a plot for his life. But the *materia* at hand, in the form of the makeshift baptismal vessel, the "clouded plastic" hospital glass, offends Will's well-bred sensibilities: "But surely it was to be expected that the priest have a kit of some sort." In a parody of Christ's agony in the garden—"let this cup pass from me"—the glass remains unincarnate, untransfigured by the leap of faith which endows something other with symbolic value. Will sees in the "clouded plastic glass" only the gratuitous insufficiency of materials which embarrasses his environmentalist expectations. The stubborn extraness of the item, its ungreetability by imagination and its immunity to synthesis, witnesses to Will's deafness to the summons to pilgrimage. He is unable to begin his life. In that deficiency he assumes the likeness of death, and in a most appropriate specific form. Reducing the mystery of death to a problem in manners, turning news, as ever, into knowledge, astonishment into inertia, Will, not death, appears at the last as the great leveler.

The gravitational pull of home is felt in *The Last Gentleman* in several ways. The word tolls throughout the book. "Take me home," says Kitty at the end of the "sniper's den" scene. I'm taking Jamie *home*," declares Mr. Vaught in New York. On his deathbed Jamie speaks "seriously of going home, no, not home but to the Gulf Coast." Will's continual expulsion from places, even in mid-occupation, as a consequent of his mediateness, begins too in the course of the book to suggest its contrary: a rehearsal for ultimate inhabitation. His very flight, that is, begins in a kind of palimpsest effect, characteristic of the novel's most important mode of disclosure, to reveal the possibility of pilgrimage. Finally, the increasing aerialization and celestialization of imagery in the novel—the sky in the desert is "empty map space"— suggest the belief that in Mircea Eliade's words, "man desires to have his abode in a space opening upward." For the home Will ultimately seeks is not in his hometown of Ithaca, Mississippi, but in heaven, and the father he ultimately seeks is no earthly one but the Father of Souls. Man's only home on earth is *the road home*. It is not a state, some plugged-in *locus amoenus,* but a status—that of a sovereign pilgrim stranger. The finally relevant question is never, where is man? but, what is man? And the finally relevant answer is not an ecology of life but a theology of being.

To this end, Will's blind, unwitting search for home is at once bound up in and set off by Percy's own quest in the novel for authority. As a Christian existentialist, Percy has communication problems that extend beyond the deadening of responses consequent to stimulus flooding and psychic overloads. His outreach as a religious writer is peculiarly crippled by contemporary exhaustion of charismatic and prophetic properties, which are reflected, as we have seen, in the leveling of place, language, and death. In addition, Christian notions of "sin" and "grace" are as remote today as alchemy or the four humors. Orthodox religious counters are simply dead issues—nonnegotiable. Will, the title character, upon whom the novel is lost—he "misses it!"—is the putative reader. Percy's altogether formidable task, as it was Flannery O'Connor's, is to make God real in His absence. God must be invoked without being named. Necessarily eschewing appeal to vestiges of man's old religious consciousness, which would reinforce spiritual indifference and make dismissal irresistible, Percy endeavors to become postmodern man's new, lost memory. To keep the religious vision in a time of trouble, to echo William Blake, Percy works with the "religious" in "its root sense as signifying a radical *bond* . . . which connects man with reality— or the failure of such a bond—and so confers meaning to his life—or the absence of meaning." Will's repeatedly missed appointments with his fundamental identity at once express directly the accelerating contemporary appetite for instant, disposable creation and obliquely an objectless, irreligious dream of God. Percy's authorial role is as decreative as it is re-creative. If man realizes his loss, perhaps he will recognize it. If he forgets being, perhaps he will discover it firsthand. Like O'Connor with her sacred blasphemies, Percy works through indirection. Harboring perhaps equal malice toward man's organized ignorance of his own nature, Percy seeks his authority in scandal.

But how to make scandalous the scandal of contemporary loss? The scarcity of scandal—any scandal—is one of the embarrassments of present-day dearth. In his nostalgia for sin and longing for apocalypse, Sutter Vaught, the novel's surrogate author, embodies Percy's need to create scandal. To this end, Percy, like Sutter, woos death. Death in the novel, as demonstrated by its progress out of the picturesque into the grotesque, is a symbol always being overtaken by reality. Death is conceived as at once the symbol and the scandal—that is, the scandalization—of man's existential absence, his missing of himself. The chaos without freedom; the end without revelation, consequent to postmodern leveling; man's outliving of himself by confusing the Bomb and the Second Coming, the survival of a body and the salvation of a soul; the reduction of love to an impersonal narcissistic attraction of emptiness for emptiness: these states Percy scandalizes by experiencing them through the novel's recollective consciousness as the sensations of a dead world body.

Intensifying its presidium over the novel's successive precincts, until it emerges in the deathbed baptism scene as a "presence," a "somebody," in the room, death is not only a scandal-monger, it is also the most visible manifestation of the author's Muse. "The consciousness requires a presence," says Percy, "in order that a literature be conceived between them." Like Yeats's antiself, death is the necessary adversary that forces the conceiving self to exceed itself. In this excess, of which scandal is but one specific form, Percy finally bases his claim to authority. His intimacy with death is the exhibited necessity of his freedom. In the character-action of the novel his artist-Muse relationship with death is subsumed in a host-guest relationship, which is all-important to the novel's shaping intentions. The politics of this relationship impose a need for ritual, and not (as Will thinks in his concern over the seemliness of the baptismal utensil) for technique. The ritual base requisite for alluding to being—our only way of expressing it—and for the reinstatement of spiritual quest is wrought in *The Last Gentleman* under the tutelary genius of death.

In his choice of a home for Will, where, presumably, he and Kitty will live after they are married, Percy passes on to Will his own exacting problem of rehabilitating leveled materials. There the trinity of resources—place, language, and death—exist challengingly in a bathetically reduced condition. The home features a "ferny dell" and a "plashy brook" (place), a "'bridge'" (language), as its former seafaring owner, Cap'n Andy, has nicknamed the ridge overlooking a plain, and, circling above, "buzzards and crows" (death). Cap'n Andy, we learn, "bored himself to death." He succumbed, that is, in Saul Bellow's definition of boredom, to the "pain caused by unused powers, the pain of wasted possibilities or talents . . . accompanied by expectations of the optimum utilization of capacities." Like Will, by and large, especially in the deathbed baptism scene, Cap'n Andy embodies the definition of entropy as energy unavailable for work during a natural process. Cap'n Andy's is a museum exhibit of leveled human resources. We are back at ground zero.

But the carefully wrought underwork of the novel, articulating the opposed imagination of news, prepares us to find latent in ground zero a possibility of the sacred center (hence the location of the former in Central Park). There Will might successfully return place, language, and death to their wonted inexhaustibility. He might successfully hold them in regenerative unity (acting out the novel's most teasing phrase—"a perfect pyramid, shedding itself"). If so, then the pigeon of entropy turns before our eyes into the dove of epiphany. With its "best view on the ridge," its open upward accesses, the place is built for the reception of news. The "bridge" bespeaks language's mediational powers and the bonding strength of the namer's faith. The circling "buzzards and crows" picture Will's gyration outward in search of his center, his true home, and symbolize the companioning ministry of death that instructs him in his alienation. This, together with the analogue of the place as a ship (it has a "'fo'c's'le'" too) and with Cap'n Andy's rank of command, suggests the continuous activation of Will's status as a sovereign pilgrim stranger. Seen thus, the place is the road home: a portable capability of self-renewal, a dynamic repose in the insufficiency of the given.

In this way the place sums up the two dominant sensations of the novel: danger and hope. The leveling of the world may become a demonic end in itself. Perversity will be felt as originality, problems as solutions, and loss, intensified, as gain. On the other hand, leveling may proceed finally to de-create man's falsified identity as a tourist and a consumer and to reveal his true identity as a pilgrim and a participant. The astonishing failure of the things in which man has misplaced himself may lead to his self-recovery. The immaculate solitudes of the desert, where we leave Will, are either the verge of extinction or the preliminary to communion. The novel is a network of uncompleted arrangements, a series of transformations held firmly, almost intolerably, in reserve. Yet the novel's very open-endedness is, in contrast to the closed system of an end game, a gesture of hope. And Will, we note, is at the conclusion of the novel less the fugitive of history (he no longer tries to avert Confederate defeats) and less the prisoner of science (he has set aside his telescope). His last word in the novel, "Wait," is the watchword of the author himself. It betokens, we can hope, an orientation at once chastened, almost suppliant, and alert, toward news. Does it suggest a nascent vulnerability to the grace to continue? Perhaps the novel is, at the end, best described as a "balance of stone—with gestures to grow."

SIMONE VAUTHIER

Narrative Triangulation
in The Last Gentleman

In "The Man on the Train," Walker Percy has evoked "the triple alliance" that fiction can establish between reader, character, and author. The experiential "triple alliance" mirrors, on a different scale, the triadic nature of language which Walker Percy has investigated in several of his linguistic essays. But it is also reflected within the text in the trinity of narrator, narration, and narratee. Since this trinity is the basic structure of narrative, as it is of discourse, obviously only wide ranging variations of the relations among the three elements distinguish different kinds of narrative. In a given story the fundamental set of relations undergoes changes as the narrator's distance to his subject and/or to his narratee increases or diminishes. The narrative triangle is never a static form, though it may be more or less dynamic. Examination of the shifts in narrational relations is therefore as important to the understanding of a novel as content analysis. Walker Percy's nonfictional work provides a special incentive to study his fiction in this light. I have analysed elsewhere the situation of discourse in *The Moviegoer*. Here I propose to explore *The Last Gentleman*. Within the limited scope of this essay, however, it is impossible to chart all the shifts in the narrational structure, and I shall merely take a few soundings to establish some of the narrator's positions in that structure.

A comparison of the beginning and ending of *The Last Gentleman* throws light on the narrator's journey on the narrational map. Although

From *The Art of Walker Percy: Stratagems for Being.* © 1979 by Louisiana State University Press.

Kierkegaard and Guardini stand double guard at the gates, the epigraphs of *The Last Gentleman* need not scare away the reader: the domain within, as one enters it, seems reassuring: "One fine day in early summer a young man lay thinking in Central Park." However wary modern fiction may have made us, we feel reasonably confident that the story will tell us who the young man is, what he is doing in Central Park, and why the fine summer day is of special importance. Is not all this promised us in the familiar phrasing and tone, the very shibboleth of the storyteller? Nor do the following paragraphs, although they modify the almost legendary lilt of the first sentence with more matter-of-fact descriptions, disappoint our expectations: they provide and withhold information about the young man in the most satisfying manner, while showing that the knowledgeable narrator is firmly in control: "In the course of the next five minutes the young man was to witness by chance an insignificant, though rather curious happening. It was the telescope that became the instrument of a bit of accidental eavesdropping. As a consequence of a chance event the rest of his life was to be changed." Yes . . . chance, change, and destiny . . . all the ingredients of a good traditional narrative.

However, the expectations aroused by the first chapter do not simply concern the content of the story but its narrational configuration as well. Clearly, the vague chronological specification, which sets the subject at some undefined and indefinable temporal remove from the narrator and the narratee, would have been in keeping with the novel's two alternative titles, *The Fallout* and *Ground Zero*. Moreover "one day" presupposes an indeterminate series of other days and the indefinite article "a young man" a background of human beings from which a selection has been made, presumably because of its significance. The beginning of *The Last Gentleman,* unlike those of *The Moviegoer* and *Love in the Ruins,* implies that the narrative discourse is a segment of an infinite narration. It suggests the remote, abstractive attitude of the narrator and the exemplarity of the particular story which is about to be told.

But who is going to tell this story? With the first sentence, some hesitation is still possible since a first-person narrator might yet make his appearance as a witness to the scene. But the rest of the page confirms the impression suggested in the opening line that we are reading a third-person narration. If the narrator is undramatized he is by no means absent. He first intervenes to evince previous knowledge of the "next five minutes" and "the rest of [the character's] life." He stresses the articulation between the near and the far future by explaining that the telescope is to be the instrument of the change. The mention of the telescope, the function of which is to transform the insignificant into the fateful, can be heard as a statement of fact. But it can also be heard metaphorically, since an optical instrument turns into a means of eavesdropping.

The narrator turns to the subject of the announced transformation: "He was an unusual young man. But perhaps nowadays it is not so unusual. What distinguished him anyhow was this: he had to know everything before he could do anything. For example, he had to know what other people's infirmities were before he could get on a footing with them." The comment, "he was an unusual young man," at once endows the character with his first explicit psychological feature, and gives the extraordinary events about to be told a semblance of realistic motivation, the common-sense assumption being that unusual things happen to unusual people. But at this point the narrator pauses. Can he really depend on such a norm? The idea that the allocutor may differ from his notion of the usual clearly impels the narrator to add an oddly concessive clause ("What distinguished him anyhow was this . . .") and to produce an "example," reasserting his right to define the young man. Phrases like *anyhow* and *for example* also show a narrator didactically presenting his information for maximum discursive effect, while the present tenses and a number of deictics call attention to the act of narration. Despite the lack of a grammatical *I* the situation created is that of discourse, or what Benveniste calls *récit,* an utterance assuming a speaker and a hearer and in the speaker the intention of influencing the other in some way. From the first page of the novel it is clear that the set of relations established designates rather than effaces its triangularity. However unspecified the locus of the narration, the locutor outlines a subject for the benefit of an allocutor. The three elements are held in balance. One might diagram the narrative configuration as an equilateral triangle.

To turn to the last section of the book is to face a narrative situation which, although basically no different, is significantly changed. Of the three terms of the narrative triangle, the subject has now come to the foreground. Apparently unaware of the narratee, the narrator, no longer accenting his act of narration, reports a conversation between Will Barrett and Sutter Vaught, limiting himself to a few stage directions and introducing only six out of forty-eight of the characters' replies. On half a dozen occasions, he tells about sensations or thoughts of the protagonist's (e.g., "His heart began to thud," and "a style of driving which the engineer faintly recalled from the 1940's"). The narrator has moved away from the narratee whom he no longer instructs and guides, closer to the hero, with whom he even seems to identify. Almost transparent, he leaves us to face the characters' words, their few gestures, or the car's shuddering to a stop, and to decipher the meaning of the scene.

(Hence the impression that the ending, as many critics and the author himself have noted, is ambiguous.) Change therefore not only occurs at the level of the diegesis but also takes place at the level of the narration, affecting the locutor-subject-allocutor triad. As the narratee's apex has receded into the background and narrator and subject have come closer, the shape of the initial narrative triangle has considerably altered.

The final narrative unit fixes the figures of discourse in one ultimate position, but the narrational balance has all along been shifting. The shifts in triangulation appear most clearly when one looks at those aspects of the narrator's function that distinguish him from more traditional narrators.

One activity sharply differentiates the narrator of *The Last Gentleman* and is instrumental in defining his standpoint—I mean his nomenclature. Take the naming of the hero. Let us grant that he was originally christened by the author. Williston Bibb Barrett is provided with a full-sounding name, including not only first name and surname but also a middle name, all of which are, in common southern fashion, patronyms. The whole name functions in the way in which proper names do in fiction—that is to say independently from the impersonal narrator but not from the narration which dictates certain kinds of names and assigns to each individual instance a place in its own onomastic system. For his part "the novelist typically indicates his intention of presenting a character as a particular individual by naming him in exactly the same way as particular individuals are named in ordinary life"; furthermore since the proper name is, as Roland Barthes has noted, "the prince of signifiers," it is rich in connotations, whether social or symbolic. The symbolic code can only be tentatively apprehended as one first hears the name: not until the end of the story can one evaluate to what extent *nomen est omen*. But the socioeconomic code is more immediately decipherable. With its three patronymic signifiers, "Williston Bibb Barrett" connotes good old "Anglo-Saxon" stock, as against such Irish names as Gallagher or Sheehan, or such continental European names as Gamow or Fava, and southern origins against the midwestern suggestions of Carol (Kerrel) Schwartz or the metropolitan sound of Morton Prince, which seems to belong to a character in a *New Yorker* story; it connotes upper-class and aristocratic breeding in comparison with such plebeian names as Bugs Flieger, Beans Ross, or Myra Thigpen. Fittingly what is recorded of the past in the hero's name is conflicting, Bibb suggesting slavery, while Barrett recalls the efforts of Lysander Barrett to have slavery abolished in the District of Columbia, and Williston a famous Harvard Law School professor.

Usually the proper name is a commodity to the author-narrator insofar as it conveniently gathers and identifies a number of semantic traits, themselves making up that word-construct, the fictional character. But, strange to say, the narrator of *The Last Gentleman* is very reluctant to avail himself of the triple handle to the character with which he has been furnished. He names the hero only twice and contents himself with designating him. This feature of the narration has not gone unnoticed, but Martin Luschei, to my knowledge, is the only critic to have attempted to explain it:

> It is instructive to watch how the author refers to him through the first chapter. Here in this homeless place he is presented as "a young man." More frequently the designation is simply "he," but in this first chaper Will's specific designations alternate between "the young man" and "the Southerner." In the office of Dr. Gamow, his analyst, he becomes "the patient" of "the other. . . ." The changing designations reflect the reality because here in New York he is a chameleon, indentified [sic] by successive functions, changing color protectively to conform to his surroundings: these are his roles. Percy weaves "the engineer" in unobtrusively a dozen times by way of preparation and actually names him Williston Bibb Barrett just before he identifies him permanently as "the engineer."

Interesting as it is, the analysis falls a little short. For one thing Martin Luschei seems to refer to the narrator's *second* act of naming. The first occurs before the visit to Gamow and deserves more attention: "For another month or so the young man, whose name was Williston Bibb Barrett or Will Barrett or Billy Barrett, sat rocking on the gallery with six women." The information—which in the third-person novel is usually conveyed much earlier—is here yielded incidentally, sandwiched in the relation of an iterative scene and by way of introduction to a list of *unnamed* but vividly depicted women, as though the young man's name dubiously guaranteed his difference. And, in truth, is the narrator really naming the hero? The willingness with which he rattles two other cognomens, the interchangeability of which is underlined by the repetition of *or,* is in fact evidence of his reluctance to fix the identity of the character, all the more so since nicknames, being situational, have not the same general validity. The surplus of names seems to point to some lack, some failure of the proper name to denote. With the exception of the one time he is again called Williston Bibb Barrett, the character will henceforth be simply designated, though the process of designation is not as straightforward as Martin Luschei indicates.

Undoubtedly, *the engineer* is, after the first chapter, the most constant appellation. But others are occasionally introduced, the most frequent being *the boy, the young man, the youth*—not to mention *he*. The hero also variously appears as *the patient, the hitchhiker, the passenger, the tutor, the interpreter, the visitor, the other,* and even *the Englishman*. (The last denomination is not literal but metaphoric in the context of the novel—for the Englishman repeatedly stands for a certain fictional and cinematographic type gifted with a capacity for both eavesdropping and survival.) Moreover the narrator keeps playing with the basic designation by qualifying it with an impressive number of epithets—*sentient, courteous, poor, bemused, attentive, puzzled, sweating, canny, mystified, shivering, prudent, forgetful, gentlemanly, flabbergasted, interested, sleepy, frowning, tactful,* etc. Now he doubles the epithets: "the poor addled engineer," "the pleasant forward-facing engineer"; now he doubles and opposes them, "the chivalrous but wry engineer," "the courteous but terrified engineer"; now he triples them, "the poor bemused shivering engineer" or he triples and opposes them "the hard-pressed but courteous and puissant engineer." These adjectives may be referential either when they define a quality of the engineer (like *sentient, courteous,* respectively referring to the aesthetic and the ethical sides of Will, and *bemused* which indicates a frequent state of mind) or else when they describe a particular response to a particular stimulus ("the frowning engineer" or "the reeling engineer," etc.). Again they may be oriented no longer toward the referent but toward the speaker, revealing the narrator's attitude ("the poor engineer"). Some may be used "straight" in one context and ironically in another.

Whatever their meaning, the epithets perturb the smooth flow of the narration. Without them the signifier "the engineer" would soon become emptier than it already is and function much in the way of a third-person pronoun, as a shifter. The adjectives, however, keep reestablishing the threatened status of the signifier and they create a subtle interplay of tensions. Since some of the qualifiers are also recurrent, some syntagms (notably "the sentient engineer" and "the courteous engineer") tend to become clichés of the narration and as such to be now obtrusive, now transparent. Roughly speaking—and leaving aside the problem of ironical use—the relation of the narrator to his subject when he employs an identical phrase seems to be the same but his relation to the narratee is paradoxical: he invites the narratee to recognize the syntagm as familiar, i.e., to accept it as both adequate, and as somehow insufficient since it needs to be repeated so often; on the other hand, repetition of the proper name, which supposedly expresses a particular identity, can have no such implications. Further, the relation of the reader to the cliché-loving narrator and his narration is slightly changed with every recurrence. Either the repetition is not perceived—the phrase *has* become a shifter—or it is perceived and then felt as redundant or meaningful, destructive or constructive. The fact that so many of the repetitions in the story included significant variations, of course, incites the reader to look for meaning in recurrence, just as the epithets modulate the use of the fixed syntagms. The designation "the engineer" therefore is like a coin the exchange value of which keeps altering as it circulates from context to context, from narrator to narratee, and from author to reader.

Such convertibility, however, is not merely the effect of what is repeated and/or added: it is a property of the token itself which the modifiers enhance. Face-up or face-down, it is not the same figure of speech. The designation can be seen as a *metonymy*: Will Barrett has a job as a "humidification engineer," that is, as "a kind of janitor." The word itself is therefore a euphemism which the narrator, together with Macy's and society at large, prefers over the more homely and humble "janitor." But if the stakes of modern technological society are clear—while it reduces the man to his function in the system of production, it nominally aggrandizes the function by blurring the outlines of its designation—the stakes of the narrator in this mystification are less obvious. Probably he is poking sly fun at our grand use of language. In any case, he is distancing himself from the hero. More important, the appellation also works in his discourse as a *metaphor* and this metaphor no longer embodies a sociolinguistic code, but echoes the very thoughts of the protagonist: "I am indeed an engineer, he thought, if only a humidification engineer, which is no great shakes of a profession. But I am also an engineeer in a deeper sense: I shall engineer the future of my life according to the scientific principles and the self-knowledge I have so arduously gained from five years of analysis." Employing the word metaphorically, the narrator would seem to accept the character's self-image. And perhaps he does on occasion. But things are in fact more complex. What with his lapses of memory, *déjà vu*'s, and "little fits," the poor engineer is in reality not able to engineer much.

That inability is precisely his possibility of salvation; for life can be managed empirically and scientifically only at the expense of authenticity, of being. Thus the narrator's use of the appellation functions as a point of irony or as a pointer to a blank: "the engineer" opens a series of empty spaces—between the word and the referential occupation, between the function and the person, between the person and his self—until they seem to riddle the narration and light a fuse chain of questions. Beyond the self—what? To sum up, "the engineer" is not a permanent identification, both because the frequent label designates no viable durable role but a void, and because the narrator occasionally changes the label. Two of his alternatives deserve consideration. "The boy" (or "the youth") occurs in those moments when the past surfaces again in the narration and a different Will Barrett is resurrected. This disjunctive device underlines the fragmentation of the agent into different actors, but the phrase "the young man" can also make the junction between the remembered and the remembering selves. "The other" is interesting because of its collocations: it appears mostly in the conversations with Sutter Vaught, when Will has become able to speak in his own name and to establish an intersubjective relation. "The other" is not the narrator's casual way to solve the narrative problem of referring to the hero; else its occurrences would be more evenly distributed. It marks the fluctuating relation of the narrator to the object of his narration who is then seen as part of a locutory situation; Will Barrett can only be "the other" in reference to someone and when looked at from the angle of an observer. The narrator momentarily ceases to use Barrett's focus of vision as he can (and often does) even when calling him "the engineer." Moreover, since Sutter is Will's Significant Other, the narrator in those final conversations seems to turn the tables and to show that both diegetic locutors have become equals from his viewpoint.

"The engineer" also resounds as an unexpected echo to a phrase which, after it is introduced in the novel, we keep looking for in vain through the text. There is a tension between the connotations of "the engineer" and those of "the last gentleman": the former connotes modernity, pragmatism, empiricism, possibility (significantly a crash course turns Will Barrett into a maintenance engineer); the latter connotes the past, a vanishing social and moral code, gentility, caste—one must be to the manner born—the end of the line, impossibility. If we take it that "the last gentleman" is Will Barrett, then the two designations define the old and the new existential postures open to him, neither of which can really help him out of his problems. But curiously, rather than between significations, the resonance is between the ever-present signifier and the *absent* one. And also between an unambiguous designation and an ambiguous one—for which of the Barretts, Ed or Will, is the last gentleman? The title also creates an empty space which the text never quite saturates, the reading process never satisfactorily fills out, since even if we choose to call *Will* the last gentleman the indeterminacy of the reference still remains. What is more, the very recurrence of the identification tag goes on widening the gap between the two designations, in symbolic reflection, perhaps, of our riven world, and in textual reflection of the nonidentity of narrator and author.

The narrator's reluctance to name the protagonist, which, I insist, is personal to him and not to be mistaken for the author's, his fondness for generic names (the actor, the pseudo-Negro, and the Handsome Woman, etc.) are part of the novel's general onomastic system. In particular, they must be evaluated against the carefulness with which he reports all the appellative courtesies used by the characters. Apart from such common terms as *man, baby, honey, son,* and Rita's esoteric *lance corporal*—the hero is variously addressed or introduced as Mr. Barrett, Barrett, Will Barrett, Billy Barrett, Williston, Will, Bill, Mist' Billy, Billy Boy, Ed Barrett's boy, Mr. Ed's boy. He is even given pseudo names which manifest joviality or playfulness: "another five minutes and they'd call him Rocky"; "They called him Bombo, the son of Tarzan and Mr. Clean. The engineer had to laugh. They were good fellows and funny." But when the supercilious actor persists in calling Will Barrett *Merle,* he betrays his own arrogant rudeness. We can say of pseudo names what Lévi-Strauss says of the use of proper names: *On signifie toujours que ce soit l'autre ou soi-même.* The multiplicity of names is undoubtedly correlative of the various, conflicting images of Will which the characters have and perhaps need. In this context both the playful nicknaming and the actor's willful confusion are grace notes which draw attention to the importance of naming and its relation to roles. For similarly, in the speech of others, Jamison becomes Jamie, Jimmy, Jimbo, Tiger; Valentine is Val, Sister Johnette, Mary Vianney, Sister Val, Sister Viney.

What's in a name? *The Last Gentleman* asks: Something of you for me? Something of me for you? But it also asks, "Under what circumstances does naming really name?" All the names conferred upon Williston Bibb Barrett fail to name him fully. In his fugue states, the hero himself cannot remember his identity. Will Barrett, whose nervous condition seems related to his father's suicide, blots out the patronym that links him to all the short-lived Barrett males. At the beginning of the story, even when remembering it, he has to have it confirmed by a card: "My name is Williston Bibb Barrett, he said aloud, consulting his wallet to make sure." His name is what it is to a child, "the name that we are told is ours." The novel is partly the story of his acceptance of himself as a subject through the free use of his name. As late as the Ithaca episode, there occurs an incident when he has to remind someone of who he is; and he says: "'This is Will Barrett, Beans . . . Mr. Ed's boy.'" The giving of his name, being mere identification for the other, ends in depersonalization: the *I* is reduced to a mirroring third person doubly reflected in the deictic *this,* which registers the gap between the speaker and what is pointed at, and in the referral to himself as his father's son. Only at the end will he be able to appropriate his name and even turn its utterance into self-affirmation: "'Dr. Vaught, I need you. I, Will Barrett' and he actually pointed to himself lest there be a mistake, '—need you and want you to come back.'" The odd gesture translates in body language, but, being centripetal and no longer centrifugal, it *reverts* the verbal "this" of the earlier incident. "For," in the words of Lewis A. Lawson, "by exercising will he becomes a self . . . and in willing one thing, Will, according to Kierkegaard, is showing purity of heart." What must be stressed, however, is that the act of will is a speech act requiring the assumption of the name of Will—a diegetic event which is highlighted by the narrational practice of designation; for now the designation "the engineer" disappears.

Avoided by a narrator who constantly privileges designation, hesitantly worn by a protagonist unprepared to endow his name with meaning, *Williston Bibb Barrett* becomes an ambiguous signifier to be decoded diversely as the story unfolds. Since the narrator has refrained from providing the narratee with clues, the deciphering becomes the reader's entire responsibility. As we first play with the name, negative suggestions come to mind: Will-is-not, will-is-not. Will a man provided with a Bib(b) be able to feed himself, to go beyond dependence on a sustaining parental figure? (Both Val and Vaught, let it be noted, suggest value.) And what a strange *bar* in the patronym! What does it obstruct?—what forbid?—what cross? But then we realize that Will-Bear-it is perhaps programmed in the name. And why not I-will-bar-it? Now that I assume my name I can lay down the law in my turn. So perhaps Will (will)-is-not-barred. Yet even at the last we feel the tug in the name, *Will* pulling against *Barrett*. An emblem of the riven self? A symbol of the tension between will, the subjective self, and a higher law that demands from man that he relinquish his personal will? An onomastic inscription of the predicament of man faced with possibility/impossibility? As it can no longer be taken for granted, the name becomes a matrix of signification, hidden yet active, which are left to the reader to name.

The functioning of names must therefore be seen in a global perspective. It is not enough to say that the changing designations reflect the reality of the protagonist's role-playing. The substitutions of all kinds also point to the drift and displacement of subject and object through the text. When he calls the hero "the engineer," or "the Englishman" or "the other," the narrator stands in a different relation to him or to his narration. By the same token, it is not enough to say that "the *novelist* distances his hero with patronizing names" (emphasis mine), since the distance must be constantly reassessed and is not really condescending; at most the narrator is mildly amused at the vagaries of the poor engineer but he remains sympathetic to his foibles and to his plight. The distance furthermore is an aesthetic effect that shapes the reader's response as much as it reveals the narrator's attitude. When it subverts the fictional convention that makes the patronym the sign for a person, *The Last Gentleman* undermines the mimetic illusion. The repetition of *the engineer,* however diversified, is like a blinking light, issuing the warning: this is a *character,* you are reading a tale. Thus it diminishes our blind dependence on the text, our willingness to accept it as representation.

To this extent, *The Last Gentleman* comes closer to avant-garde fiction than *The Moviegoer.* However, the narration here only undercuts the representational value of the novel in order to enhance its poetic truth. The dysfunctioning of names does not work toward a dissolving of the concept of person or toward what Walker Percy would call a "loss of the creature." It rather throws into relief their potential functioning. Proper names appear to be not only signs but symbols of being; they have the power of all names freshly used to "bring about a new orientation toward the world." Not that names can symbolize me or you; but they symbolize that I am and you are, and on this basis we can establish an intersubjective relation—and perhaps a relation to being. In the extended naming process that is the novel, a dynamic movement orients Will Barrett away from engineering and reliance on cards in his wallet toward self-autonomy and true dialogue, and similarly directs the reader away from unthinking identification with the protagonist, or absorption in a "reflection of life," toward an active role in the exchanges that are taking place.

Another activity of the narrator leads to greater or lesser modifications of his angle in the narrative figure: when he (re)-produces a character's discourse, whether oral or mental, the narrator is obviously closer to him than when he describes him or narrates his actions. (Indeed the very bulk of conversations in the fictional web of *The Last Gentleman* is in itself significant, all the more so since this emphasis is not a necessary development of the initial narrative situation. Of course it powerfully contributes to the elaboration of the themes—the theme of the quest, which is a quest for the Word, and the theme of the increasing difficulty to act meaningfully.) Whether the narrator conspicuously asserts his control over the reproduced discourse or surreptitiously effaces himself behind the characters' words depends on his choice and handling of relays of speech. If we take even the simplest case, what we may call the conventionally reported dialogues, i.e., those in which the inverted commas duly allocate ownership of utterance, we see that the narrator runs the gamut of possibilities. At one end of the spectrum, there are the long stretches of verbal intercourse in which the various utterances are left unassigned without as much as a *he* or *she said.* In such passages, the mediation of the narrator is almost invisible, although the inverted commas are, in a sense, his guarantee of literality.

In other passages, such as the conversation at the end of the eighth
section of Chapter 4, narrative mediation obtrudes heavily. Often the narrator intervenes in an effort to reproduce more than the verbal content of
the conversation. He may translate in his comments the unspoken intentions
of the speaker: "'No, it's not the game,' said Rita, gazing steadfastly away
but patting Jamie's arm with hard steady pats. Kitty's gambit didn't work,
she was saying." He also may make a consistent attempt to render the tone
and quality of voice of some of the locutors. One or another speaks in a
"loud voice, all squeaks and horns," "in a low voice," "through his teeth,"
"in anguish again," "sternly," "earnestly." He records the bodily gestures
or facial expressions accompanying the utterance: "still patting." "Rita ran
a hand through Jamie's hair," "twirling his keys glumly," "actually holding
his head." He registers the pauses and silences: "he could not bring himself
to say anything," "Sutter sighed," "Jamie groaned," "asked Rita after a
moment." Or he stresses the speed of answers: "said Jamie instantly and
soberly." He carefully notes the orientation of the locutor: "Rita, speaking
for some reason to the engineer," "looking around for the adversary," "he
glared at Rita angrily," "looking behind him as if he was expecting someone."

Thus the situation of interlocution can often become as important as
the utterances themselves. The care with which the narrator specifies the
global situation renders us as sentient as the protagonist who, listening to
Rita, "took her import not from the words she said but from the signals."
While the narrator uses the whole spectrum of possibilities for reporting
direct speech, he often locates himself at either end, instead of either mixing
the two techniques or privileging one, as is more usual. Now with the omis-
sion of all tags, he tiptoes into the wings, taking the narratee with him and
leaving the characters onstage in splendid isolation. Now with great consideration for the narratee he specifies the situational context of each speech
act through a wealth of details; and playing stage manager, author, and
director, he upstages the characters. The sharp contrast of the two methods
emphasizes his flexibility and above all the nature of the narrative structure,
the changeability of the narrative triangle.

The narrator can further perfect his vanishing trick when the conversations are not conventionally reported. For instance, section 12 of
Chapter 2, after starting abruptly with "Kitty said"—a mention which is
recalled only once a few lines later—transcribes a lengthy dialogue between
the girl and Will Barrett without the benefit of single quotation marks and
without any connective comment; thus one may wonder whether speech
attribution must be ascribed to the subject or to the narrator. In any case

the use of free direct discourse which reaches the reader without any apparent mediation, syntactical or typographical, is common practice throughout the novel. While it always makes the narration more transparent and brings the subject to the foreground, it may have diverse effects depending on the contexts.

When it is employed within ordinary direct discourse, it may give the impression of a close-up:

> "But seriously now, here's the proposition," she said. And he found that when she gave him ordinary directions he could hear her. *As of this moment you are working for me as well as for Poppy. Perhaps for both of us but at least for me. Keep Jamie up here long enough for Larry to give him a course of huamuratl. . . . Now when you get through with Larry, take Ulysses and take off. Go home. Go to Alaska. In any event, Ulysses is yours. . . . Here is the certificate of ownership, which I've signed over to you and Jamie. It will cost you one dollar. Jamie has coughed up.* She held out her hand. "I'll take my money, please" (emphasis added).

The italicized sentences in free direct discourse stand out from the rest of Rita's utterance as though seen under a magnifying glass. Yet paradoxically because their literality is not certified in the usual way they somehow have less authority than the opening and closing statements; they seem to be filtered through the subject's consciousness. Fairly often, the nonliteral free direct discourse is employed to distinguish spoken from nonspoken thoughts: "'Who? No.' *If he needed a good shaking, Sister, you should have given it to him.* But he said: 'Do you like your work here?'" Here the emphasis is authorial; and the free direct discourse seems to reproduce the more authentic thoughts of the speaker. Similarly it can also underline the intent behind the words: "'Do you know what that joker told me last night?' (This is the way we speak.) 'I always horse around with him.'" Or free direct discourse can be employed to stress the meaning of silence itself: "Jamie dispensed himself and paid no attention: *I'm sick and I don't have to oblige anybody.*" One might call this the stereoscopic effect because it discriminates between the two kinds of reported discourse, inner and outer, or two levels of narration, certified and uncertified. In all such cases the narrator provisionally disappears yet ends in making us aware of his knowledgeability, perhaps his omniscience.

If sometimes free direct discourse renders a character's inner speech with more immediacy and greater idiosyncracy, sometimes on the contrary it generalizes the inner speech in a soft-focus effect: "The engineer looked at the other as the half second wore on. You may be in a fix and I know that but what you don't know and won't believe and must find out for yourself is that I'm in a fix too and you got to get where I am before you even know what I'm talking about and I know that and that's why there is nothing to say now. Meanwhile I wish you well." Will Barrett has just met on the street a Negro, "a young man his own age" whom he presumably used to know but to whom he has nothing to say. The incident describes the new quality of race relations. Free direct discourse here makes the reflection both concrete yet impersonal and the *I* is the generalized *I* of philosophical discussion.

Finally one might speak of a dissolve effect when the use of free direct discourse permits the superimposition of one person's utterance over another's:

> As he got change from the cashier . . . [Will] began to grieve. It was the shame of it; the bare-faced embarrassment of getting worse and dying which took him by surprise and caught his breath in his throat. *How is this matter to be set right?* Were there no officials to deal with the shame of dying, to make suitable recompense? It was like getting badly beaten in a fight. To *lose.* Oh, to lose so badly. *Oh, you bastards living so well and me dying,* and where is the right of that? Oh, for the bitter shame of it (*lose,* the author's italics; other emphases added).

Through the flexible weaving of free indirect discourse and free direct discourse—emphasized in my quotation—a voice is heard which at first is clearly Will Barrett's. But then another voice—Jamie's voice—comes through. Because of the unobtrusive shift of pronouns made possible by this method of rendering inner speech, Will's monody becomes Jamie's lament, and modulates into a lyrical cry whose subject is mortal man, rather than a particular individual.

Unmarked free direct discourse occasionally tends to blur the contours between the character's and the narrator's discourses sending ripples through our image of the narrative triangle: "It *was* like home here, but different too. At home *we have* J. C. Penney's and old ugly houses and vacant lots and new ugly houses. Here *were* pretty wooden things" (emphasis added). The blurring is all the more important in the case of questions because then the addressee changes: "The puzzle is: where does love pitch its tent? In the fine fervor of a summer night, in a jolly dark wood wherein one has a bit o'fun as the English say? Or in this dread tenderness of hers?" This is probably a rendering of Will's thoughts and the question therefore is self-addressed, but some hesitation is made possible by the tense of the introductory verb, "the puzzle *is*," so that the narratee (and thus the reader) is also invited to ponder about the nature of love.

Needless to say, a similar blurring is often obtained through the reproducing of thoughts or utterances in free indirect discourse. Since for long stretches at a time the focus is internalized and the viewpoint is that of Will Barrett, it is at times difficult to ascertain whether the narrator immediately records what the hero sees or mediately reports his consciousness of what is being seen. Hence the mistaken idea of one reviewer that Barrett is the narrator, or the more percipient remark of Benjamin DeMott that the narrator is an alter ego of the protagonist. These views however discount all the passages in which the narrative agency relays the *thoughts* of other characters, as illustrated in some of the examples above, or renders *collective thoughts*. (One of the best of many possible illustrations is the description of the Vaught servants in the third section of Chapter 4, which mixes commentary, free indirect discourse, and free direct discourse in a prose as subtle as its subject.) In short our brief study has proved the narrator's interest in *situations of language,* his resourcefulness in reproducing them, his pliancy in selecting the parameters to be excluded or included, the wide range of degrees of his interposition. Even through his role as relay of speech, therefore, the narrator is able to modify the angles of the narrative triangle.

Examination of the shifts in viewpoint also emphasizes the narrator's mobility on a larger narrational scale. All possible narrative stances are represented in the text in varying proportions. The narrative instance is now within the character's consciousness, now behind him but close by and lacking superior knowledge, now outside him and in a position of knowledge. In the last instance, he is not averse to passing judgments on the hero: "He had, of course, got everything twisted around. Though he took pride in his 'objectivity' and his 'evidence,' what evidence there was, was evidence of his own deteriorating condition." Faced with such assessments, however, we may feel inclined, possibly urged by the narrator, to qualify his own assertions. (The above quotation goes on: "If there were any 'noxious particles' around, they were, as every psychologist knows, more likely to be found inside his head than in the sky." The generalizing explanation, "as every psychologist knows," is suspicious especially to anyone familiar with Walker Percy's thinking; the statement about the noxious particles being "in his head" is scientifically dubious in its present formulation.) But commentaries crop up throughout, for instance in the recurrent tag "the engineer who always told the truth." The narrator will even briefly map out the protagonist's future near the end of his story, thus providing the reader with a major clue: "Perhaps this moment more than any other, the moment of his first astonishment, marked the beginning for the engineer of what is called a normal life. From that time forward it was possible to meet him and after a few minutes form a clear notion of what sort of fellow he was and how he would spend the rest of his life."

In a sense, of course, the vagaries of the narrator correspond to those of the hero. Since Walker Percy wanted to present Barrett's "symptoms" "equivocally" he needed a narrator who would not be wholly consistent. That these contractions and expansions of the field of vision alter the rapport of the narrator to his subject needs hardly to be stressed—except to suggest that the alteration powerfully contributes to the more realistic tone of Jamie's death scene. That they modify the terms of the triple alliance established between author, reader, and narration deserves more attention. Even a third-person narrator can prove unreliable. How are we to trust one who diversely identifies himself with the lost protagonist—and with great success too as in the episode in Chapter 5 with the nurse when "all at once time fell in"?— yet who is also careful to mark his distance from the protagonist? (The narrator even feigns ignorance in Chapter 3 of where the protagonist spent the night.) The legitimacy of the narrator's role seems to be impugned, and the authority of the narration called into question. The variableness of the narrative agency opens a series of gaps between the text and the reader which accounts for some of the early reviewers' uneasy response to the book.

Yet while he shares in the duplicity inherent in all narrative instances, the narrator of *The Last Gentleman* is about serious business. Witness his constant irony—the mask of a commitment to values. Witness the considerable space he devotes to Sutter's thought-provoking, indeed provocative, notebook. His own didactic penchant is manifested in the numerous phrases that articulate his narration, serving as guide-posts to his narratee: "no doubt," "anyhow," "to be specific," "strange to say," "if the truth be told," "strangest of all," "no wonder," etc. Also his didacticism appears in many evaluating commentaries and generalizations: "In hospitals we expect strangers to love us."

The story is obviously directed toward a narratee who is crucial in determining the balance of the narration. Of necessity his figure is not entirely clear-cut, either. At times it seems to become double, as in one of those old badly printed color pictures, when a sentence can be ascribed either to the narrator or to the character: "He had of course got into the Yankee way of not speaking to anyone at all. In New York it is gradually borne in upon one that you do not speak to strangers and that if you do, you are fairly taken for a homosexual." A study of the pronoun *you* in the novel would show how its extension can vary. The *you* can be a generalizing *you*: a familiar equivalent of *one,* it embraces both the character and the extradiegetic narratee who could have, or has had, a similar experience, as in the above example. Or the *you* is generalizing but intradiegetic as in the description of Lugurtha the cook who "spoke to you only of such things as juvenile delinquency"; it makes of the narratee one of the fictional people since they alone can converse with Lugurtha. In the following example things are more complex: "Yet it fell out, strange to say, that when he did find himself in a phone booth, he discovered he had spent all but nine cents! Oh damnable stupidity and fiendish bad luck, but what are you going to do?" Is the narrator assuming his commentator's role, as "strange to say" suggests, and is he then addressing the hero—an intradiegetic narratee—in mock pity, or is he taking an extradiegetic narratee to witness? Is the narrator rather reporting the character's inner monologue, in which case Will is talking to himself alone, and the narratee is metadiegetic? Or is he thinking of himself and anyone in the same circumstances, which makes the narratee both meta- and intradiegetic? The very indeterminacy of the allocutor is a textual effect which we must respond to.

Although I cannot draw here a full portrait of the extradiegetic narratee, let us note that like his partner in the act of narration he is a man of wide knowledge. The very numerous comparisons which are supposed to help him picture or imagine things more vividly imply that his own "radar" is finely attuned to Western culture in general (e.g., Mort Prince in Levittown is "like Descartes among the Burghers of Amsterdam"; a housewife is a "regular La Pasionaria of the suburbs"). The radar is also attuned to American culture, past and present, middle brow and high brow, and to southern life and mores in particular. Indeed the narratee must be as familiar as Will Barrett with the Civil War to pick up the allusion to the ancestor who died in The Crater or to the controversy about General Kirby Smith, or the ravine in Central Park which is like a sniper's den, that "Brady photographed six weeks after the battle." Phrases like "they were Sewanee episcopal types," "an equable lower-South episcopal face," "the peculiar reflected style of the deep Delta," an Alabama voice as "ancient and visible and unbuttoned" as Tallulah Bankhead's—all assume that the narratee knows about southern types, voices, nuances. He equally remembers enough of the life of the saints to appreciate the simile that has Barrett plunge "into a brierpatch like a saint of old" or turn to money as saints to contemplation. Moreover what narrator and narratee share is not simply a body of knowledge but a language. In this regard the numerous clichés serve not only as subject-oriented word pictures that describe the character through mimicking his particular cant, but also as addressee-oriented meeting-points where narrator and narratee (or reader) can communicate and commune in derisive dissociation from stereotyped speech and stultified life.

This encyclopedic shared knowledge ranging from Abou Ben Adhem to Wittgenstein and Woody Woodpecker is of course counterbalanced by the narratee's total ignorance of the hero's adventures—wherein he differs from the narrator. Although an effort of imagination is sometimes enjoined upon him ("Take an ordinary day in New York. The sun is shining." "Imagine their feeling"), native curiosity is more usually attributed to him. So the narrator relays and answers his questions: "What happens to a man to whom all things seem possible and every course of action open? Nothing of course." Should he wonder, "And Kitty?" the next paragraph will supply the information. Sometimes the narrator queries the narratee in his turn: "he'd have struck out for St. Louis (the question is, how many people nowadays would not?)," "Has not this been the case with all 'religious' people?" Thus the likeness between the narratee's fundamental situation and that of the character is hinted at while his distance and difference are recognized. More curious still are the questions which could be the narratee's and which are answered seemingly by the character: "There is the painting which has been bought at great expense and exhibited in the museum so that millions can see it. What is wrong with that? Something, said the engineer." In this way an internal dialogue is set up within the text, between the figures of the narrative triangle.

Briefly, the narratee is expected both to recognize the truth of what he is being told and to take a critical attitude toward it. He must evaluate possibilities, existential attitudes, draw analogies between the familiar—the assumptions and information he shares with the narrator—and the unknown, the lostness and dislocation of this particular hero who only becomes predictable at the end of the story. But of course the comparisons end in throwing as much light on the "happiness" of the South (or the "homelessness" of the North) or the modern post-Christian world as on the protagonist's "symptoms." Thus the presence of the narratee does not annul the vacillation created by the narrative agency, but it counterpoises it in two ways: first, insofar as it underscores the link between the fictional universe and the outside world, it precludes any interpretation of the story as merely a tale or a game played with and against narrative rules. Second, it outlines for the reader a possible perspective. If there is one figure of the narration with whom we are invited provisionally to identify, it is that of the narratee. We have to test the familiar against the unfamiliar, the unfamiliar against the familiar until, it is to be hoped, we grow in wisdom or at least become aware of our ignorance. To the reader, the slight estrangement of the whole fictional universe is a further heuristic challenge which I leave to the thematic critics to meet. It seems to me that the tale is told not in exchange for our immersion in the fictional world, our willing suspension of disbelief but rather for our *questions,* our engagement/disengagement, in exchange for our *desire.* Desire to know (but to know what?—the face of Death?—the face of God?). Desire at any rate to be.

In any case to insist on the credibility of the narrator is finally to ask for realistic representation whereas the function of the narrator in *The Last Gentleman* is eminently poetic. Far from being discredited by his changeability, he appears as the unnamed Namer who constructs a world like ours and unlike ours, sets his action in a time that may be ours or 'an as yet unnamed era," who makes us cohearers of a polyphonic universe of language. The narration counterpoints a number of voices; they echo, contradict, or answer one another in an incessant dialogue that goes on, as we have seen, even within the narrative triangle. Walker Percy is close here to the "dialogism" of Dostoevsky. An ironic but not unkindly ventriloquist, the narrator weaves an incredible number of fashionable cants into a highly idiosyncratic triumph of mixed styles, cultural clichés, social vacuities, and intellectual absurdities until they recover a lambent pregnancy, and we become convinced that we have been hearing a unique, prophetic voice. A mythic creator, the narrator points to his own begetter, the occulted author. Just as the designation "the engineer" served as a pointer to the narrator, the narrative chain reduplicates both the alienation of origins and the permanence of the Other in the act of speech. In addition, the narrator's shifts from presence to copresence to seeming absence become significant, perhaps symbolic. They generate the sense of another absence, the desire of another presence.

In this light, rather than the telescope image, the most pregnant structural metaphor for *The Last Gentleman* is the baptism scene to which the novel leads up as its harrowing climax and effulgent core. With the priest bearing God's news to Jamie, and Will interpreting Jamie to Father Boomer, the episode dramatizes a double process of mediation. Through the two overlapping triads a circulation of meaning and being is established between the diegetic participants. Similarly in the extradiegetic triple alliance that unites author, character, and reader, the reader is made to share in an exchange which may link him to "the silent Word" beyond the novelist's words. Just as the action leaves the hero groping toward a new orientation, free to accept or not "the message in the bottle" that has thus indirectly reached him, so the narration leaves the reader wondering about "what happened," free to resonate or not to "the unspoken word, the Word unheard / The Word without a word, the Word within / The world and for the world."

Whatever our personal interpretation of the novel, *The Last Gentleman* impels us not only to participate in the construction of its meaning but to do some thinking of our own about language, about the relationship between words and things and people and being. In *The Moviegoer* the narrator-protagonist was absorbed in the wonder of naming. In *The Last Gentleman* this activity is one which the narration, largely through the manipulation of the narrative triangle, demands from the implied audience. Walker Percy's concern with "Naming and Being" may therefore be less evident in his second novel; but it is no less profound.

JEROME C. CHRISTENSEN

Lancelot: *Sign for the Times*

Walker Percy's *Lancelot*, a very peculiar book, engages the critic, challenges his stance, in the way few contemporary American novels any longer care to do. *Lancelot* is the monologue—now obstreperous, now canny, now frightening, now pathetic—of a madman, the tale of a brutal negative quest, brutally told. Mad Lancelot surely is, but mad in a fashion that blunts the critic's diagnostic instrument and subverts his presumption of sane and sanitary distance, for the symmetry between the narrator's violently obsessive quest for meaning through his telling and the critic's zealous and equally over-determined pursuit of meaning in the tale is inescapable and disturbing. Is it not mad to monograph on a madman's monologue? That question identifies the predicament that is *Lancelot*—a predicament especially pointed for criticism but implicated in any authentic reading of the novel. *Lancelot* is a novel about a character in a predicament; ultimately that character is I—reader and writer.

Most Americans are well acquainted with the disadvantages of madness: the delicate wariness that settles in on the faces of relatives and friends; the irksome difficulty in keeping the golf card straight; a certain moroseness that taints one's enjoyment of even the most tasteful serials on PBS; a persistent itch beyond the power of Downy Fabric Softener to allay. But if we are almost tediously familiar with the disadvantages of madness, perhaps we are insufficiently aware of its advantages. Chief among them is the possibility

From *Walker Percy: Art and Ethics.* © 1980 by *The Southern Quarterly.* University Press of Mississippi, 1980.

of a vantage, a point of view. It may be a slight vantage, as narrow as the view from the window of a madhouse; but, as Lancelot Andrewes Lamar, madman, attests to his silent interlocuter, "the narrower the view, the more you can see." What Lancelot sees out the window of his New Orleans madhouse is "a patch of sky, a corner of Lafayette Cemetery, a slice of levee, and a short stretch of Annunciation Street," and, he tells us, part of a sign. It reads:

Free &
Ma
B

For the madman the fragment lures speculation. Lancelot freely conjectures what the whole sign might say: "Free & Easy Mac's Bowling? Free & Accepted Masons' Bar?" He expects to learn the answer when, after finally proving his sanity, he leaves his confinement. And maybe he will, though the novel ends in the delay of that departure and that discovery. I won't ever know what the complete sign says, unless I should be very lucky and on a future trip to New Orleans find such a sign on such a street. What a bonus for sanity that would be! The narrow view of the novel divulges only a partial sign, however, and, in doing so, simultaneously poses and answers the riddle, when is a sign not merely a sign? The answer: when it is a message, when it addresses me in my predicament, even if its only address is "you are in a predicament"—when, that is, I am forced to make use of it because I have nothing else. In my predicament as reader of this book, provided with only a narrow view between its red walls, the insignificant breaks upon me with the force of a message, even if that message conveys only the urgency of my questions: *Free* and what? What does *Ma* have to do with it? *B*? What? How? This must be madness.

Free &

Freedom, as Lancelot's favorite song says, is just another word for nothing left to lose. Lancelot's madness began with the sudden awareness of that freedom in the shocking recognition of nothing. From his vantage in the madhouse Lancelot tells his story, the tale of a Louisiana lawyer in his forties, squire of the family mansion of Belle Isle, a former happy hedonist whose pleasures have lost their savour. Lancelot's second wife, Margot, has made a rapid transit from *nouveau riche* to *nouveau* antiquarian; she begins by restoring Belle Isle to its antebellum splendor, tries to restore her husband to a likeness of Jefferson Davis, and turns, finally, to the project of restoring herself to a factitious glamour by becoming a motion picture actress. As if by the logic of that restoration Lancelot has been eased out of the revived grandeur of his ancestral home into the pigeonnier outback, where he roosts, a lone pigeon, while a flock of Hollywood moviemakers on location nest in the manse. Always a creature of habits, Lancelot has by now been reduced to just three: drinking, reading Raymond Chandler, and, preeminently, monitoring the news. Every pleasantly pickled hour he listens to the reports on the radio, and every evening his last, ritualistic act is to cast a blood-dimmed eye on the television's spectral summary of the day's events: no-news from everywhere. He does not realize his compulsiveness or his discontent until, one afternoon, he suddenly *does* receive news, from a wholly unexpected source, in a form not immediately explicable but immediately meaningful. The message: nothing. Or, to be more precise: oh, cipher, zero. Looking up from a Chandler novel, Lancelot glances at a release form for his daughter's summer camp and notices that her blood type is listed as I-0. That 0, the place-saver in the decimal system, when placed behind the one and the hyphen, simultaneously indicates his daughter's blood-type and displaces Lancelot with his IV-AB from her blood-line, involving the giddy inference that he has been replaced in his wife's bed. Lancelot retrospectively compares the effect of this discovery to the insistent and catastrophic chain of inferences that follow upon an astronomer's observation of the dislodgment of a single point of light in a galaxy trillions of miles away: "The astronomer sees a dot in the wrong place, makes a calculation, and infers the indisputable: comet on collision course, tidal waves, oceans rising, forests ablaze. The cuckold sees a single letter of the alphabet in the wrong place. From such insignificant evidence he can infer with at least as much certitude as the astronomer an equally incommensurate scene: his wife's thighs spread, a cry, not recognizably hers, escaping her lips. The equivalent of the end of the world following upon the out-of-place dot is her ecstasy inferred from the O."

A violent logic, which will, for Lancelot, justify violence. Violent, but if mad, it is the madness of our own Judaeo-Christian culture, which becomes intelligible only in the plausibility of the end of the world and in the possibility of moral and spiritual equivalents to the eschaton. And, given the end of the world, a certain violent logic does enforce itself: because the eschaton will be a unique and totalizing event, it must be incommensurate with anything else, context or cause. For both astronomer and cuckold to follow the chain of inferences that unveils the end of the world requires a transcendental leap from the general to the unique, from evidence to experience, from mild interest to fierce passion. It follows that the truest moral equivalent to the eschaton emerges where incommensurability is both most familiar and least intelligible, in the sexual climax, which, as Lancelot argues, belongs to none of our conventional categories and which is, properly speaking, *unspeakable*. The incommensurability of the sexual orgasm, which in its *ek stasis* takes one out of one's place, opens to an absolute beyond the phenomenal—an absolute, Lancelot insists, either infinitely good or infinitely evil. The only anchor available to stabilize this indeterminate moment is fidelity; fidelity between the partners to this grave ecstasy is the life preserving fiction of a benign commensurability. For Lancelot to suddenly infer the entirely separate ecstasy of his wife from the out-of-place, unfaithful O is to cut away that stabilizing anchor and to chart will he nill he a course to the end of the line: to sheer negativity, absolute evil. Such is the logic of eschatology, wherein the world is ultimately consumed not because of a stray comet but because of its own incommensurate, fatal significance.

Suddenly, giddily free, with nothing left to lose, Lancelot seems to come to himself, feels capable of action for the first time in many years. The inference of absolute evil does have, like madness, its compensations: it makes knights out of broken down old boozers, and it imparts a kind of heady joy in the heart of despair—what Lancelot calls a "secret sweetness at the core of dread." Lancelot describes that peculiar emotion by comparing the discovery of his wife's infidelity to the time when, as a child, he accidentally came upon a cache of 10,000 embezzled dollars buried beneath the argyle socks in his father's bureau—evidence of an unsuspected corruption that knocked the son's world to pieces. He recalls the hunger of his eyes for the sight of that dirty money, how they shifted to and fro ever so slightly, scanning, gluttonously trying to take it all in. Lancelot feels the same sweet dread in the evidence of his wife's ecstasy. Opening to his eye, the O provokes what Lancelot calls the "worm of interest," which, once stimulated, will wriggle into an emptiness at one and the same time repellent and inviting. For the worm, inference is but appetizer. Though vengeance be Lancelot's goal, he must satisfy the interested eye by feasting on the act itself in the absolute knowledge of whether all is good or evil, niceness or buggery.

In his pursuit of this awful knowledge Lancelot eccentrically emulates the method of Philip Marlowe, tarnished knight in the city of fallen angels. The man becomes the private I; private eye turns peeper. He first enlists the services of his black factotum Elgin (the name of a watch) to observe and chart the comings and goings of the film crew at the local Holiday Inn. When the evidence of bedhopping proves inconclusive, Lancelot, with the help of Elgin's MIT-trained expertise, sophisticates his methods, substituting for his servant's eyes the objective probing lens of the camera. After insuring that the film company will have to spend their last two nights at Belle Isle, he converts the house into a weird television studio, each bedroom equipped with its own prosthetic eyeball. But the more sophisticated the equipment, the more bizarre the results. This technique of bringing the sinners into focus with movement-activated cameras and infrared lenses does show them compromised but in a compromise of the viewing instrument itself, which records them strangely distorted—a so-called negative effect that aptly comments on Lancelot's negative quest.

Furious to eliminate the indeterminacy that haunts him, Lancelot decides to feast his eyes directly on the truth. He prepares for a vengeance that will be identical with knowledge, where the hidden evil will be raped by a sovereign knower. The next evening he diverts gas from a partially capped well into the ventilation system of the sealed house and then balefully enters its poisonous darkness. The cold eye of the hurricane that rages without, Lancelot pierces ever deeper into the bedrooms of those who sport in adultery and perversions, until, at the center, he ruthlessly lances the infections with penis and knife in a violent knowledge that discloses the secret of life and affirms the justice of his quest even as the apocalyptic explosion of the gas-filled house affirms the intelligibility of history itself.

Apocalypse may have come, but Lancelot, survivor, is no less haunted. By recounting his terrible story to a priest/physician and former friend he seeks to regain a lost focus and assurance, to rediscover a truth he is sure he knows. In this narrative quest the mind wends its way through a lurid landscape oppressively charged with significance. The madman's compact with lover and poet is to compare great things with small. And as Lancelot has inferred absolute evil from the evidence of his wife's infidelity, so does he find in his predicament the type of an evil that has correspondences everywhere. Whether or not the world has actually ended or will end, the need for an end and for a new beginning is starkly legible in the signs of the times. The madman's litany of those signs builds to a wholesale denunciation of the homogenized hell of contemporary America; "Washington, the country, is down the drain. Everyone knows it. The people have lost it to the politicians, bureaucrats, drunk Congressmen, lying Presidents, White House preachers, C.I.A., F.B.I., Mafia, Pentagon, pornographers, muggers, buggers, bribers, bribe takers, rich crooked cowboys, sclerotic Southerners, rich crooked Yankees, dirty books, dirty movies, dirty plays, dirty talk shows, dirty soap operas, fags, lesbians, abortionists, Jesus shouters, anti-Jesus shouters, dying cities, dying schools, courses in how to fuck for schoolchildren."

The loss of the country is the surrender to spectacle; the task of living has become a business of show. And show business—Hollywood movies and moviemakers—becomes for Lancelot the epitome of a pervasive, disgusting infidelity of appearance to reality. A century ago Walt Whitman stood on California's shores and saw the great westering circle almost circled. Just twenty years ago Allen Ginsberg wandered through a supermarket in California and found *both* peaches *and* penumbras. Today, Lancelot envisions a California where a movie theater playing *Deep Throat* snuggles knowingly up to the gates of San Clemente—the Hollywood version of Paradise, where the hypocrite will lie down with the pornographer. Worse, in the inevitable reflex of sin, Hollywood, with its hurricane machines and freeze-dried divinities, has spread east, where actors and actresses, producers and directors mindlessly spout the ideology of a joyful, life-enhancing sexuality while they secretly practice fornication and buggery in lewd daisy chains that are the perversion of nature. As it must, the diseased part infects the whole: Lamia—fantastic, alluring—first poisons the bed and then one's hold on reality itself: "The world had gone crazy, said the crazy man in his cell. What was nutty was that the movie folk were trafficking in illusions in a real world but the real world thought that its reality could only be found in the illusions." The proper equivalent of this nutty indeterminacy is not the liberal's daydream of a pluralist society fondly tolerant of all distinctions, but Pandaemonium, Mammon's mimic kingdom—a hellish nightmare which threatens to make all distinctions impossible. One choice alone remains: to settle into that ultimate form of alienation that Blake called the limit of opacity or to elect a Luciferian indignation which in acknowledging a fallen estate insists nonetheless on the prerogatives of a proud sovereignty.

As his indignant answer to this intolerable age of Sodom Lancelot envisions a new order of things where sovereignty is possible, a place and time of capable action. He prophesies a revolution. "You have your Sacred Heart," he tells the priest. "We have Lee. We are the Third Revolution. The First Revolution in 1776 against the stupid British succeeded. The Second Revolution in 1861 against the money-grubbing North failed—as it should have because we got stuck with the Negro thing and it was our fault. The Third Revolution will succeed." Lancelot's prophecy corrects the American myth of the ever new frontier by identifying it as the mere rotation of keenly felt, constrictive limits with the comforting illusion of the limitless. In its stead he projects a myth of return, to Virginia, beautiful island between North and South, where America began, where will congregate a band of gentlemen, militant in their assured virtue, disciplined by the knightly values of "tight-lipped courtesy between men. And chivalry toward women," whom the men will save "from the whoredom they've chosen." The stern Virginian will fashion from *Free & O* (open, type 0, type and archetype, aught and naught) the noble prospect for a sanely limited community. Lancelot quotes inspiringly from the traditional song:

> Oh, Columbia, our blessed mother
> You know we wait until you guide us.
> Give us a sign and march beside us.

The curve of Lancelot's madness is the impassioned trajectory from the misplaced *0* tickling his worm of interest to this vision of Columbia chastely offering a transparent sign of noble purpose to her marching sons.

And what of Columbia's daughters? What will their freedom be? Lancelot is explicit: "They will have the freedom to be a Lady or a Whore"— a single, determinate choice, on which the whole vision rests, for that determinacy is anchored in the great secret of life which was the unholy prize of Lancelot's quest. "The great secret of the ages," he reveals, "is that man has evolved, is born, lives, and dies for one end and one end only: to commit a sexual assault on another human or to submit to such an assault." He goes on later: "God's secret design for man is that man's happiness lies for men in men practicing violence upon women and that woman's happiness lies in submitting to it." Given that brutal design, the distinction between lady and whore is simply a reflection of the determinate difference between fidelity and betrayal. The news that in this fallen world such a distinction can and must be made is the grail that Lancelot has brought back from the end of the world. As an answer to the priest's pious objection that we have been redeemed, Lancelot disdainfully gestures to his narrow view and says, "Look out there. Does it look like we are redeemed?"

Can this view be controverted? Try. It's like arguing with a madman. A madman with a sword. Would it do any good to suggest that this vision of a reactionary revolution is actually a repetition, to point out that Southern men have already banded together as a clan of knights sworn to chivalric protection of the pure Southern Lady? Almost certainly not, for in his madness Lancelot knows what we Sodomites do not guess, that in the hazards of true repetition lies the only possibility of raising alienated consciousness to the second power, a secondary reflection which in its difference identifies the mind's potential sovereignty and freedom. This power of repetition is attested to by the major repetitions in the book: the repetition of the quest of the original Lancelot by his namesake; the repetition of the quest of the latter-day knight in his monologue. One must return in order to begin. In repetition is the possibility of action and knowledge.

But repetition is also the limit of action and knowledge. One can plan a Virginian garden of Adamic freedom; but, as we know, the limit of Adam is Eve. Lancelot chooses as his Eve, Anna, the woman in the next cell, who has been reduced by gang rape to near catatonia and whom he involves in various fantasies of communication and conjugation. When recovered, however, she shatters those fantasies in her climactic rejection of his vision of Gentleman Adam and Lady Eve, sovereign raper and submissive rapee. "Are you suggesting," she cries, "that I, myself, me, my person, can be violated by a *man*? You goddamn men. Don't you know that there are more important things in this world? Next you'll be telling me that despite myself I liked it." Her angry response, proclaiming an absolute resistance to violation by a self open to more important things, disrupts the delicate focus of Lancelot's monologue and repeats a disturbance that, he realizes, occurred earlier—on the night of his vengeance and in the heart of his triumph. There, at the end of the line, his unfaithful wife Margot, the ark of covenant that bears his unholy grail, speaks to him in a poignant, etherized dismay about the losses of their lives. Just before the final conflagration she asks, "What's the matter with me?" "What?" he responds. "That's what you never knew," she says. "With you I had to be either—or—but never a—uh—woman. It was good for a while." Her last words are less important than her last silences. The rapee turns on the raper in the moment of his knowledge with a gentle accusation that is the dying echo of a lost possibility: you never knew; I had to be either—or—but never a—uh—woman. The pauses mark the limits of Lancelot's knowledge: either a lady or a whore but never a woman. And what he hears, he sees. In the flaring of the last match Lancelot can see his wife in the corner "lying on her side," as he tells it, "like Anna, knees drawn up, cheek against her hands pressed palms together, dark eyes gazing at me." At the end of the line the knower looks into the sweet secret of dread and sees that secret looking back at him.

The limit of Adam may be Eve, but what does

Ma

have to do with it? The limit of Lancelot, as we know from Malory, is Lancelot, who is both his virtue *and* his taint. The unexpected memory of Margot and the rejection by Anna rupture Lancelot's narrative like the return of the repressed, releasing the confession that his quest had failed after all, that he never found the secret knowledge he has professed. Instead of whore or rapee he has come upon a woman staring at him in sympathy or shouting at him in rage—each encounter marking the beam in his own hungry eye. This failure and its consequent repression occur because this hero is not only Lancelot but Lancelot Andrewes Lamar, son of a dreamy, impotent country squire who just happens to be a crook, and of Lily of Belle Isle, frail and pretty, who just happens, it seems (the evidence is inferential), to be an adultress with jovial Uncle Harry. As Lancelot repeatedly recalls, the primal scene of infidelity lay in his childhood discovery of the dirty money hidden in the cavity of his father's sock drawer, the moment when he first experienced the wild surmise that would later prompt him to his unholy quest. But what of Ma? As it was his mother who sent him (wittingly or unwittingly?) on that first unknowing journey to the uncanny secret—sign of dishonor and impotence—in his father's drawer, so it is his mother who appears in a vision as Joan of Arc to offer him the sword, or at least the Bowie knife, of vengeance at the fatal hour. But if it is his mother as Lady whom Lancelot is avenging, it is also his mother as Whore on whom he is taking vengeance. For it is his mother's uncertain fidelity which is the type of that indeterminacy between Lady and Whore that Lancelot aims to extirpate. He rouses himself from a stupor like his father's and attempts to save himself from the emasculation involved in his father's substitution of the bundle of bright, green money for the fact of a female sexuality too darkly, sweetly dreadful to confront. In attempting to free himself from his father's impotent trance, however, Lancelot obsessively repeats his father's self-destructive evasions. Fantasizing his mother as Joan of Arc, militant virgin, and accepting from her hands the prosthetic penis of the Bowie knife is an arming every bit as unmanning as his father's disarming retreat into genteel avarice. If his father dishonored himself by substituting the corrupt image of money for the uncanniness of his wife's cunt, then Lancelot repeats that error in his substitution of the fascinating uncanniness of the cunt for the vital indeterminacy of the woman. The measure of Lancelot's ambivalence is the impossibility of a man ever knowing absolutely whether his mother is a lady or a whore. The motive of his action is the incapacity of *this* man ever to accept her as a woman. By finding and sacrificing the actual whore, be it Margot or Hollywood, he hopes to save the memory of his mother—Joan of Arc, Columbia, America herself—as Lady. It never works.

Now I *am* in a predicament. I can, if I choose, yield to the momentum of my argument and reasonably explain away Lancelot's rant by psychoanalyzing him, reducing his unsettling vision of America, of man and woman, to the wholly understandable consequence of childhood trauma. From that perspective all that stuff about the end of the world is merely more of the same. Repetition is the limit of action and knowledge. But the monstrous excellence of this book is that though Percy generously supplies the material and tools for such a reduction, he cannily prohibits any comfort in its execution. If I, rationalist, substitute a bright, tidy psychoanalytic explanation for Lancelot's eccentric narrative, I merely repeat his obsessive quest for the determinate and thereby commit myself to a monologue mad like his but chilling and sterile. Every man has a Ma, but only Lancelot tells this disturbing story.

Repetition is the possibility of action and knowledge. That possibility is realized in the book through the development of the figure who listens to Lancelot's story. A priest/physician, what Lancelot calls either "screwed-up priest or half-assed physician," he is a childhood friend of Lancelot's, who has been known by many names. Called Percival, for the knight "who found the Grail and brought life to a dead land," he visits the tomb of Lancelot where he must both discover and exercise his powers of rejuvenation. Called Pussy, he represents the hard chance that man may come to terms not only with woman but also with the femininity that is part of his own make-up. Called John, he must identify himself as either "John the Evangelist who loved so much or John the Baptist, a loner out in the wilderness." While listening to Lancelot this man, "neither fish nor fowl" when the monologue begins, passes from a state of abstraction to an exploratory interest, and finally to a difficult commitment both to Lancelot and to a renewed religious faith—a commitment quietly signaled by the priest's hesitation in the cemetery outside Lancelot's narrow window as he stops, stoops, to pray for the dead: for Lancelot, for himself, for me. Percival does not bring his grail to a dead land; he *finds* his grail in the broken quest and the tormented narrative of Lancelot. The priest/physician who aimed to give therapy receives instead news of, in, and for his predicament. And what he receives he charitably returns. When Lancelot, in the madness of his lucidity, light without warmth, exclaims that he is cold, it is John the Evangelist who responds, not simply to comfort Lancelot in his chill, but to rescue him from what the poet of *Paradise Lost* called "the bitter change / Of fierce extremes, extremes by change more fierce, / From Beds of raging Fire, to starve in Ice / [His] soft Ethereal warmth." The priest responds to Lancelot's implied question,

B

be what? how?, with the promise of a message, of good news.

That news is never spoken. But the signs of the text, however partial, support, even demand a conjecture. The news must be the hardly possible alternative to both the intolerable Sodom of contemporary America and the mad, murderous rage of Lancelot. It is the alternative that the priest has been advancing all along: first automatically, then guiltily, then cautiously, and, finally, with an authority that leaves Lancelot and the reader hanging on his words: love. Love earned by ordeal, offered in risk, justified by a mortal need. Not *just* love, but *Christian* love. Lancelot had justified his quest for sure knowledge of pure sin as a negative proof of God. "If," he had said, "there is such a thing as sin, *evil,* a living malignant force, there *must* be a God" (italics added). The new sovereignty of man that Lancelot had envisioned would have been the earthly analogue of the stern dominion of a divine father. Absolute knowledge forestalled, so is the sovereignty of God and the certainty of his potent justice. But the indeterminacy that remains, clarified by trial and refined by need represents the existential possibility of Christ and his redemptive love: a love whose incarnation is the revived fraternal affection of Percival for Lancelot, and whose prospective images are the charity of a priest in Alabama and the family of man, woman, and daughter in the mountains of Virginia.

That message of love is, as I've said, not spoken in this text. Indeed Lancelot has contemptuously commanded his Percival, "Don't speak to me of Christian love." The priest obeys; he speaks only a series of reassuring "yeses" at the close, affirmations that are not statements but *acts* of love. Perhaps the message of love cannot be spoken without being rendered as utterly banal. And though it is part of the critic's job to make banal utterances, I do apologize for mine. We can't be too certain, or perhaps I should say certain enough, about this book. Like Lancelot, who does not find the consubstantial sign of evil, who can no longer expect the transparent sign that Columbia has promised her sons, and who never even acts on his determination to leave his cell to finally learn the complete version of

Free &

Ma

B

we must take our messages from broken signs, which may madden us or make us lovers—perhaps madden us *then* make us lovers—in a world which, read rightly, is always balancing precariously between a catastrophic end and a tentative beginning.

I have referred to the monstrous excellence of this book, hardly a novel. The text does open like a novel, pricking the reader's worm of interest and inviting him to penetrate the core, to repeat Lancelot's quest for a final knowledge: reader as raper, book as rapee. But the blandishments of structure and motif betray such a reader; what he finally glimpses is something quite different from the feast he had anticipated. Shockingly intolerant of the conventional enticements, radically skeptical of the sources of its own power, this book rebukes the reader's easy interest and shatters his pretense of detachment by involving him in a repetition of Lancelot's catastrophe, a repetition that is the limit and the possibility of readerly action and knowledge. Fiction and tract, narrative and harangue, *Lancelot* is a book that collapses under the pressure of its message. In its collapse *is* its message. Like the priest who learns a saving love from the disjointed monologue of a madman, I, reader and writer, chastened in my pride, subdued by the "end of the novel," can perhaps hear in the silence of the text an urgent note of distress. This note is not the call of madman or prophet but the plaintive, warning song of a canary.

DOREEN A. FOWLER

Answers and Ambiguity in Percy's The Second Coming

With *The Second Coming* (1980), Walker Percy is trying to deliver answers. In a recent interview, he suggested that the work, his "first unalienated novel," represents a departure or breakthrough in his literary career: "I'm convinced that in *The Second Coming* there's a definite advance, a resolution of the ambiguity with which some of my other novels end: the victory, in Freudian terms, of eros over thanatos, life over death," (Walker Percy, an interview with James Atlas, *New York Times Book Review,* 29 June 1980, p. 30). In *The Second Coming,* Percy is making a deliberate attempt to avoid ambiguity, to do more than merely satirize contemporary mores, to offer answers and state them plainly. In the past, critics have frequently complained of Percy's penchant for equivocation and especially of his tendency to write indecisive and even enigmatic endings. Such indecisiveness has given rise to diverse and sometimes contradictory critical opinions as to the fundamental world view that informs Percy's fiction. Some critics have interpreted Percy's novels as expressions of Christian faith, while others have maintained that Percy takes a despairing, even nihilistic view of life. With *The Second Coming,* Percy is responding to this critical confusion; he is trying to make his affirmations plain.

Despite Percy's effort in *The Second Coming* to state his answers clearly, his tendency to opacity is not entirely overcome. Try as he will to offer constructive criticism, to suggest alternative modes of living, to root out the source of the modern malaise, Percy's very manner of presentation frequently

---

From *Critique* 23, no. 2 (Winter 1981–82). © 1981 by James Dean Young.

seems either to defuse or to invalidate his answers. A fundamental ambivalence polarizes his fiction as Percy tries to make his art stretch to straddle
two widely disparate views of life—a heroic, idealistic attitude and a more
practical, empirical position. Because Percy refuses to commit himself entirely to one view, his answers are often contradicted by opposing suggestions
in the novel, creating a precarious balance of opposites.

The Second Coming, Percy tells us, is the story of two people, Will
Barrett and Allison Huger, who "achieve their lives." At the beginning of
the novel, both Will and Allison are having trouble living; both have, more
or less, quit. Allison has taken refuge from the world in a mental institution,
and Will, recently widowed and worth about fifty or sixty million dollars,
is contemplating suicide. All this soon changes; Will and Allison are about
to learn how to live. Allison escapes from the mental institution and charts
a new, independent life in a greenhouse. Will, deciding he must have some
answers, goes to a cave where he waits for a sign from God—or death—
whichever occurs first. A toothache cuts short Will's cave-experiment; and,
while trying to find his way out of the cave, he falls into Allison's greenhouse.
Soon Allison and Will are in love.

Percy's least ambiguous answer—a forceful rejection of escape—is even
clear in this cursory plot summary. Because the business of living, easy
enough for some, has always daunted and nearly defeated Percy's analytic
protagonists, escape has appeared as a seductive temptation in his fiction,
as it has in the fiction of at least one other Southerner. Faulkner's characters,
like Percy's, have typically found attractive two methods of shirking an unsatisfactory existence: suicide and passive abdication. In *The Sound and the
Fury* Quentin Compson kills himself in rejection of a world where honor,
pride, and truth seem to have no resting place. In *Light in August* the Rev-
erend Hightower chooses a less flamboyant means of escape—he merely
retires from life. In *The Second Coming* Will Barrett fluctuates between these
ways of repudiating life and finally rejects escape in favor of its opposite—
a firm commitment to act, work, and live.

Throughout *The Second Coming* Will toys with the idea of suicide. If
life is "senseless and farcical," why not then swiftly and cleanly end it? Will's
father had committed suicide and at one time, so Will believes, tried to kill
both himself and his son. At the conclusion of *The Second Coming* Will
rejects his father's solution. In a Holiday Inn room, with Allison lying beside
him, Will hears his father's voice: "Make your own bright end in the darkness of this dying world, this foul and feckless place, where you know as
well as I that nothing really works, that you were never once yourself." Will
rises in the dark, dresses, and walks to his car. He removes from the trunk

his father's Greener and his own Luger. In an act of ultimate repudiation, he hurls both guns into a gulley: death is not an answer—his resolution to live is unmistakable.

Will also rejects the other seductive path: evasion of life. One need not commit suicide; one can simply wait life out, sitting idly on the sidelines. In many of Percy's novels, sedentary abdication figures as an enticing alternative to life. Lancelot Lamar sits in his pigeonnier, waiting for the six-o'clock news; Binx Bolling sits life out in movie theaters; in *The Second Coming* Sutter Vaught watches M★A★S★H while he waits for retirement, and Will, early in the novel, realizes that up to now he has missed his life, the way a man might miss a plane.

Before the end of the novel, when Will finally commits himself to seeking his life, he has one last relapse into passivity. After his stay in the cave, he returns home, and his daughter, doctor, and spiritual advisor take charge of his life. Will passes these days as others have dictated, wearing a robe and slippers, shuffling about a convalescent home, watching the Morning Movie. The convalescent home is easier but just as lethal as Will's father's bullet through the mouth, and ultimately Will rejects this form of death, too. Outside the sheltered, structured existence of the home, "the fresh cold air felt good in his face" and "things took on significance." Will heads toward Allison, a job, and life.

Allison is Will's counterpart in *The Second Coming,* and her story, point for point, matches his. Like Will, Allison had tried to relinquish her life and, like him, rejects defection in favor of commitment. While Will had considered suicide and idling away his life, Allison seeks escape in madness: she no longer has to meet the glances of others and sits under tables, rather than at them, confronting knees rather than faces. Madness is a ticket to escape, for it voids her responsibilities to other people: "Sometimes she thought she had gone crazy rather than have to talk to people." Early in the novel, Allison, again like Will, shoulders the burden of her life. Instead of taking instructions from others, Allison follows "Instructions from Myself to Myself" and successfully directs her escape from the mental institution. Allison's liberation from Valleyhead corresponds to Will's liberation from the convalescent home. Both are choosing freedom with its concomitant responsibilities; both are taking charge of their lives. At Valleyhead, Allison's life was managed entirely by others (even the decision to shock her brain was made by others), while in the greenhouse she rejects all help, refusing to allow Will to help her move the giant stove. By hoisting the stove from the ruined house to the greenhouse, Allison proves that she can shape reality to meet her needs.

At the end of *The Second Coming,* Allison and Will, two people who had shunned the world, are planning a return and re-entry. They resolve to marry in a church and send their children to public schools; to build low-income houses, incorporate, and profit-share. All such plans herald a triumphant return to the world of cooperative living with others. Percy's solution is clear: man must eschew escape and live among the human community, fostering and supporting man's institutions. It is a wise-sounding plan but not a feasible one, given the world Percy has created. He advocates commitment to society, but the society he pictures is an inferno of sordid passions and discontent. Of all the characters in *The Second Coming* only the two main ones and Father Weatherbee, who is tacked on like an afterthought at the end, are spared from caricature. All the rest, the society members with whom Will and Allison mean to live and work, are lampooned. Percy captures and conveys the essence of these characters with a single apt phrase: Father Jack Curl does not use deodorant, and a tuft of bronze hair curls through the zipper of his jumpsuit; Jimmy Rogers gets too close when he speaks and has stuff between his teeth; Marion was good and decent and a wheelchairful of ocherus fat; Ewell McBee corners Will in the coatroom of the Holiday Inn—he wants to "neck-rassle"; Leslie's forehead is permanently dented with an inverted U—the sign of her perpetual discontent; and Kitty clunks gold when she moves—the sign of her avarice. Can Will and Allison "achieve their lives" attending PTA meetings with people like these? One is strongly disposed to think not.

Conceivably, Will's perception of society's members is distorted. Will's friends and family may not be greedy, corrupt, and dissatisfied; perhaps they only appear so to Will. We see the world through his eyes, and the narrator tells us that Will is crazy. If we discount Will's views as psychotic, what view does the novel offer? We have Will's world or none; there is no alternative. And despite the narrator's warnings, Will does not appear insane. His thoughts are logical, and his criticisms of society valid. Will seems not crazy but intolerant. He tends to see other people the way Gulliver saw the Brobdingnagians—with their flaws exaggerated. Whatever the source, the overriding problem—the reader's inability to accept the possibility of survival and success within society—remains the same. Whether the cause is Will's intolerant view of people or the people themselves (and the reader tends to think it a combination of both), the novel gives no hint that either will change. Without some improvement in either Will's point of view or the empty and aimless world he sees, Will's and Allison's pledge of allegiance to the human community must seem doomed to failure. For this reason, then, Percy's answer of commitment lacks persuasiveness. Even as Percy urges man to join the ranks of humanity, his presentation of those ranks suggests that he is dissatisfied with and discouraged by mankind's inadequacies. On the surface, Percy proposes a pragmatic approach to humanity's problems: man should accept what is and work within the system. Beneath the surface, Percy idealistically longs for a better world.

Percy's answer of commitment to society seems dubious for still another reason. Implicit throughout *The Second Coming* is the suggestion that society deadens life, that only outsiders, those who live apart from the human community, are still vital. The living dead surround Will—his father, quoting Matthew Arnold, had called them "the ignorant armies that clash by night"—and the only characters who seem to possess some measure of vitality are those who are least enmeshed in society: Will, who is "always dropping out"; Father Weatherbee, who spent fifty years among the Philippine natives and no longer understands his own people; and Allison, who is a stranger to the world as a result of electroshock treatments. Percy's characters seem whole and healthy exactly in proportion to their estrangement from society. Allison, for example, is most remote from the modern world—she is Percy's Miranda, a new Eve, and remembers practically nothing of the past—her own or her culture's. To convey Allison's apartness, Percy invokes images of estrangement. She is like Rip Van Winkle, like a child raised by wolves, like one who has lived alone in the mountains. Allison is untainted by society and, not coincidentally, strong—a hoister who can lift Will, the contaminated modern man, when he falls. Her very language is an act of revivification; she breathes new life into old dead forms. Allison is Will's salvation, and significantly she is as foreign to the modern world as a creature from another planet.

Haunted by the specter of living death throughout the novel, Will renounces death in all its many forms at the end and looks to Allison and Father Weatherbee for life. The young girl and the old priest seem like oases of health on a dying landscape, but Will's hope does not come from within— it comes from outside of society. Even as Percy prescribes commitment to society, he pictures only sickness and discontent within the boundaries of civilization. Once again, the power of Percy's answer is muted by conflicting claims.

Commitment is, however, only one of Percy's answers in *The Second Coming*; knowledge is another. Like the many headed hydra, knowledge sprouts two questions for every answer. In the novel Percy tries to answer questions by setting up working definitions of knowledge; knowledge is having a chance: "Knowing about what is going to happen is having a chance to escape it. If you don't know about it, it will certainly happen to you. But if you know, will it not happen anyway?" Knowledge is necessary for action but not necessarily sufficient for successful action; knowledge is man's chance to shape reality to his will. How much knowledge is enough to take action? How can a man act when he knows so little, almost nothing, about the nature, purpose, and ultimate end of his existence? In *The Last Gentleman* (1966) Will Barrett thought he "had to know everything before he could do anything." Was he right? His cave-wait is an attempt to find answers to these questions. In the cave he seeks ultimate knowledge—knowledge of God. If God shows Himself, Will has his answer and knows how to live; if God refuses to show Himself (or does not exist), he will, not knowing how to live, die.

At first glance, Will's cave-experiment seems an unqualified failure; a toothache relieves him of metaphysical longings and forces him out of the cave. On closer analysis, the outcome of the experiment yields a number of only partially concealed meanings. Looking for God in the cave, Will (literally) falls across Allison. Percy has placed her in a greenhouse built into the side of a mountain beneath a cave for a specific purpose—so that Will should stumble across her while looking for God. Percy is implying a substitution—Allison/love for God. Will was looking for a manifestation of God and found Allison, who offers the possibility of love. Perhaps love is our access to God? Perhaps love is the sign of God's immanence in the world?

Still other possible answers are implied by Will's cave-wait. His search for knowledge in a cave inevitably recalls Platonic philosophy, for the cave was Plato's metaphor for human existence: man lives in a dark cave, far from the light, and sees only dim, distorted shadows on the cave wall. Such reference to Plato's cave suggests a possible answer: man's inability to see the truth does not necessarily mean that the truth does not exist. A number of images which connote an innate human blindness reinforce the inference. Allison puts it this way: "Imagine being born with gold-tinted corneas and undertaking a lifelong search for gold. You'd never find it." The problem, then, may not be in the external world but in man. Perhaps God is immanent in the world, but human eyes cannot detect His signs. Human blindness or weaksightedness is frequently acknowledged in *The Second Coming*. Allison is like "a little cave bat," a creature unaccustomed to the light; and Will's father, who abjured an unsatisfactory life by committing suicide, is the "old mole," who chooses to bury himself in the earth rather than seek out the light. Such images all carry the same implication. The truth may be evident but invisible to weaksighted humans.

Percy's answer raises another question. If men are blind, how are they to live? Percy is ready with an answer. Though blind, the bat can fly, the mole can burrow, and man can live. Will learned in the cave that one can and must act despite limited understanding. When asked about the success of his cave-experiment, Will responds with an unqualified affirmation—he found the answer he was looking for. Asked what the answer was, he replies, "I don't know." What Will does know is "what to do." His cave-wait was successful in this sense; he has his answer. He knows as much as a man needs to know—he knows what to do. He can act; he can live.

By a different route, Allison makes the same discovery; she can act without complete knowledge. While in *The Last Gentleman* Will had wanted to know everything before doing anything, Allison acts effectively knowing almost nothing. Electroshock therapy has practically extinguished her memory, making her a virtual newcomer to the world (when Will falls into her greenhouse, she wonders if a plummeting man is a rare, but not surprising, occurrence in this strange, new world). Despite her lack of knowledge, Allison successfully arranges the greenhouse and acts effectively even when she does not understand the meaning of her act. When Will asks Allison to send a telegram "straight message," she is mystified by the expression but dutifully repeats it to the telegraph operator who understands the meaning even though she does not. Man need not know all to act; all he needs to know is what to do.

In *The Last Gentleman* Will would settle for nothing less than absolute knowledge; in *The Second Coming* he is still delivering ultimatums to God. He waits in the cave to find God or die, and he is chastised for his presumption. Will's fall from the cave is reminiscent of the fall of Icarus; like him, Will is overreaching; he is flying too close to the sun and is summarily returned to his place—the earth of Allison's greenhouse. God will not be hounded out of hiding, and those who try will fall. Will's fall, then, is a reminder of man's limitations and a lesson in acceptance of those limitations. It is enough, Percy implies, to know what to do.

One of Percy's answers in *The Second Coming*, then, is acceptance of man's limited knowledge. Man should get on with the business of life without all the answers. The problem with such advice is that Will Barrett cannot take it. Like all of Percy's protagonists, he needs to know. He questions as naturally as he breathes; wonder is his nourishment. Will's name labels him as a seeker—Will Barrett wills to bare it; he is determined to unveil the hidden truth, sharing with all of Percy's heroes a will to understand. In *The Moviegoer* (1961), Binx Bolling has his search—his ongoing quest to understand the universe; in *The Last Gentleman*, Will Barrett dogs Sutter Vaught's footsteps, determined to find out what he knows; in *Love in the Ruins* (1971), Dr. Thomas More searches for a new world of happiness; in *Lancelot* (1977), Lancelot Andrewes Lamar looks for evidence of a moral order; and in *The Second Coming* Will waits in a cave for word from God. All of these characters are distinguished by the same quality—a formidable thirst for knowledge. They weigh, question, hypothesize, and interpret every word, gesture, and posture in an unending quest for meaning. For them, life is a search.

The Second Coming counsels acknowledgment of man's inability to see. Despite the lesson, Will is pursuing absolute knowledge at the end of the novel as relentlessly as ever. Having failed to locate God in a cave, he now looks for God in an old priest: "Could it be that the Lord is here, masquerading behind this simple silly old face?" Father Weatherbee seems "to know something"; from him, Will can learn the truth. Though the novel has implied the futility of seeking ultimate knowledge, Percy's hero cannot give up the search. The lesson of the novel unnoticed, Will Barrett follows truth to its lair. The close similarity of the endings of *The Second Coming* and *The Last Gentleman* indicates that the lesson of acceptance of limited knowledge has had no impact on Will's behavior. At the conclusion of the earlier novel, Will is running joyously after Sutter Vaught's Edsel with "a final question." At the end of *The Second Coming,* no less joyous, Will is clinging to Father Weatherbee, searching the old man's face for a sign from God. Will cannot give up the quest for ultimate meaning; he cannot stop looking for God. He must continue to try to make sense of life—yet the novel has suggested that the senselessness is a given, the condition of man's existence, with which man must learn to live.

The force of Percy's answers are mitigated by equal and opposite strains in his novel. He advocates commitment to the world as it is, and at the same time he castigates the world for falling far short of his ideal. Percy counsels acceptance of limited knowledge, but his hero is by nature a seeker, for whom inquiry is inseparable from existence. In effect, each of Percy's affirmations is countered by an opposing philosophical position. The truth, he seems to suggest, is a collage of contradictions. Such contradictoriness, or philosophical tension, can perhaps best be understood as an expression of the conflicting demands of immanence and transcendence—two terms Sutter Vaught uses in *The Last Gentleman* to describe Will's dilemma. By immanence, Sutter means man's sense of himself as part of the world of experience. By transcendence, he refers to man's sense of himself as transcending the quotidian. Will is subject to fugue states—fits of transcendence—in which he loses hold of the world of sensation. Will's problem is that he "wishes to cling to his transcendence" and at the same time "to traffic with immanence." According to Sutter, such an attempt is self-defeating; transcendence and immanence cannot be reconciled.

Like Will Barrett, Walker Percy seems to be trying, consciously or unconsciously, to reconcile immanence and transcendence. Again like Will, he seems to find the two postures immiscible. Percy advocates immanence but refuses to give up transcendence. One should, he teaches, dig into the here-and-now and take hold, abjuring visions of the impalpable. Percy counsels acceptance of an imperfect world. Man should do what can be done, work within the system, or, as Binx Bolling puts it, "listen to people, see how they stick themselves into the world, hand them along a ways in their dark journey and be handed along, and for good and selfish reasons." It is, Binx explains, the "only one thing" he can do—and Percy agrees with Binx. But Percy persists in another notion: while advocating immanence, he pursues transcendence. His protagonists, Will and Allison, sense their elevation, dislocation, and separateness from the things of this world. They ask metaphysical questions; abstraction suits them. Percy knows that a man is lost unless he can plant his foot solidly in the earth, but he cannot surrender the notion that man can also touch the sky. Two contradictory definitions of man, then, inform *The Second Coming*. Man is a finite creature, who should cast his eyes no higher than the boundaries of his world; and man is an infinite creature, whose gaze should penetrate the high seat of heaven.

In the end *The Second Coming* is not ambiguous but ambivalent. Percy is poised between contradictory and seemingly mutually exclusive truths. Man is by nature a seeker with an undying need to know, but limited knowledge is the condition of his existence. Man demands a better, purer world; but existence is itself contingent upon acceptance of what is. It is right and necessary that man acknowledge the limitations of his existence; it is equally right and necessary that man should not. Given a multiple-choice question, Percy would have to answer "both of the above." Each answer is valid; neither is complete without the other, yet each seems to deny the other. Try as Percy will to clarify and to offer resolutions, the dilemma remains, inherent in Percy's perception of existence. Truth is many sided, and Percy is caught between truths. The empiricists are right, but so are the visionaries. Neither answer satisfies Percy without the other, so both appear in an uneasy equipoise.

PATRICIA LEWIS POTEAT

Percy as Storyteller

Walker Percy's second novel, *The Last Gentleman,* begins with this sentence: "One fine day in early summer a young man lay thinking in Central Park." This young man, we soon learn, is one Williston Bibb Barrett—also known as "the engineer"—a Mississippi native and a most amiable if somewhat abstract individual. We soon learn, too, that he is not entirely well and suffers frequent "spells" during which he is liable to forget his own rather impressive name and wander for weeks at a time amongst the Civil War battlefields of Virginia and other similarly haunted places. Barrett is also possessed of an uncommonly acute "radar," a mixed blessing in that it not only helps him to know what other folk are about (often before they know it themselves) but also makes him especially vulnerable to attack by the "ravening particles," certain zinging, noxious particles which clog the air and come between our young man and his tenuous hold on reality. Thus is he reduced to careening about old battlefields paralyzed with anxiety and amnesia. The prognosis is not good.

Much like the Martian in "The Delta Factor," the ravenous particles are an important conceit in *The Last Gentleman.* Appearing like birds of ill omen whenever some especially despairing business is afoot, the particles seem to steal the very substance from both objects and persons, leaving them washed out and, in the case of the latter, prey to vague anxieties and bereft

From *Walker Percy and the Old Modern Age.* © 1985 by Louisiana State University Press. Originally entitled "Percy as Storyteller: Or, How to Avoid Getting Zapped by the Ravening Particles."

of any sense of sovereignty over their lives. While his peculiar sensitivity enables him to "see" the particles and therefore know why he feels so bad, Barrett is by no means their sole target. On the contrary, everyone suffers their deadening effects, the exact nature of which becomes clear early in the novel when Will visits the Metropolitan Museum of Art. There he finds the air "as thick as mustard gas with ravenous particles which were stealing the substance from painting and viewer alike." Despite the correct lighting, proper frames, etc., the paintings are "all but impossible to see. . . . The harder one looked the more invisible [they] became." As for the museum patrons, they are even worse off, as Barrett observes:

> From his vantage point behind the pillar, he noticed that the people who came in were both happy and afflicted. They were afflicted in their happiness. They were serene, but their serenity was a perilous thing to see. In they came, smiling, and out they went, their eyes glazed over. The paintings smoked and shriveled in their frames.

Suddenly and quite literally out of the blue, help comes in the form of a workman who falls from a skylight far above. Miraculously unhurt, he, Barrett, and a family nearby are covered with finely powdered glass. No less miraculously, the ravening particles are instantly dissipated and both persons and paintings regain substance and become visible again. As he and the family minister to the workman, Barrett chances to look up:

> It was at this moment that the engineer happened to look under his arm and catch sight of the Velázquez. It was glowing like a jewel! The painter might have just stepped out of his studio and the engineer, passing in the street, had stopped to look through the open door.
> The paintings could be seen.

It would seem, then, that one way to "get around the ravenous particles" is to have a workman fall upon you from a museum skylight. If, however, this cure seems more dangerous than the disease, there is another less perilous therapy implicated in this scene, one that has to do with the role of the storyteller as theorist. On the heels of the passage above, the narrator observes, "He had, of course, got everything turned around. . . . If there were any 'noxious particles' around, they were more likely to be found inside his head than in the sky." In one perfectly obvious sense, we could dismiss the alleged existence of the ravenous particles as merely another symptom of Barrett's illness. While we might be clinically correct to do so, to leave it at that would be to overlook the real significance of this episode both in terms of *The Last Gentleman* per se and of the more catholic concerns of this essay. Quite apart from the question as to whether the noxious particles are "inside his head" or "in the sky," the scene in the museum not only discloses what Percy is about in *The Last Gentleman* but, more important, may be read as a parable of what it means alternately to take up the philosophical essay and the novel or story as an instrument for reflection. As such, this episode comprises a framework from which we may conveniently attend to the larger issue of Percy's effectiveness as a theorist of man in a narrative context.

How are we to interpret this parable? First we must recall two points made earlier. . . . I observed that the Greek word for knowledge, *epistēmē,* whence the English *epistemology,* means literally, "a placing of oneself in the position required for." Knowledge, then, and, by implication, all our feats of knowing require that we dwell in the world in a particular way; hence our way of knowing and our way of being are congruent and cannot be separated. Later, . . . I argued that truth is dramatic and agonistic; that its apprehension arises in that space of appearance created when one person speaks and another listens and speaks in turn; and that this space of appearance is the dwelling place of reality itself. Now, with these points newly in hand, think again about the scene in the museum. The difficulty facing Will and the others is at once an epistemological and an ontological one. Coming between persons and persons, persons and paintings, the zinging particles have the effect of at best clouding and at worst blotting out altogether that space of appearance without which the reality of individuals and paintings alike evaporates, bereft of its habitation. Thus deprived, each person is profoundly isolated and reduced to a perilous, glassy-eyed "serenity." To echo Arendt, nothing around them possesses that reality guaranteed by the presence of others. Instead, the world and they in it have a dreamlike quality, coming and passing away without substance or reality.

This is the situation which obtains until the workman falls from on high. It is not, however, entirely seamless. His radar going at full power, Will's place in this before-the-fall scene is different from that of his fellows, and that difference provides a clue as to why the great crash is so restorative. Central to the engineer's strategy for besting the noxious particles is that he place himself in a certain position relative to the others in the room—e.g., behind a pillar or, figuratively, on someone's shoulders. This "trick" as he calls it enables him to at least momentarily "get around the ravenous particles." In epistemological terms, we might say that, as a knower, Will stands in relation to the world quite differently from his peers. This is because he has chosen a certain framework in accordance with which his understanding of the world unfolds. Moreover, this framework is felicitous insofar as it empowers him to recognize the serenity of his peers for what it is, empty and perilous. Thus he literally and figuratively "places himself in the position required for" seeing persons and paintings as they actually are.

To borrow a phrase from *The Moviegoer*'s Binx Bolling, Will is definitely "onto something." As Kierkegaard might put it, his is the advantage of the despairing man who knows he is in despair. Our young man's hold upon this advantage is not at all secure, however, and "tricks" notwithstanding, he soon bends to the awful weight of the noxious particles. "It was," the narrator tells us, "all he could do to keep from sinking to all fours." Why is Will unable to sustain his resistance? It is because that epistemological framework which empowers him in one respect constrains him in another; or, more to the point, the indications and standards imposed by that framework are such that they effect a decidedly *in*felicitous change in his being. Specifically, the engineer makes a mistake analogous to that of Martian-novelist-Percy in "The Delta Factor." Barrett's instinct that to make sense of the human world one must look at it from something other than the same old tired perspectives and think about it with something other than the same old tired conceptual tools is quite correct. Throughout the novel this instinct stands him in good stead, but only up to a point. In the pinch, he goes astray in the same way as does Percy-as-Martian. Priding himself on being "scientifically minded," Will confuses an appropriate detachment from old perspectives and old conceptual tools with the inappropriate and godlike detachment of the Cartesian philosopher-observer. Of course, the unassuming engineer would never consciously aspire to such dizzy heights; he has enough trouble just remembering who and where he is. Nevertheless, almost everything about him—his aimless and solitary life; his amnesia; his most prized possession, a powerful, German-made telescope; his peculiarly abstracted "love" for Kitty Vaught; and perhaps most telling, his favorite role, that of an English detective consummately skilled in the art of dispassionate observation—attests to his fundamental ontological state as one who watches and listens and sees but who never commits himself through speech and action to another person.

In short, for all his acuity, friendliness, and basic decency, Will's relation to the human world is unhappily like that ascribed by Percy to Helen Keller—i.e., he is no more than tenuously connected to that world through word and deed. Thus deprived of any space of appearance in Arendt's sense, his hold on reality is finally no more secure than that of the sundry folk he spies on from behind a pillar or from some imaginary detective's burrow in Somerset.

In the idiom of W. H. Auden, "His person has become a fiction; [his] true existence / Is decided by no one and has no importance to love" (*For The Time Being*).

Wherein lies the efficacy, then, of the great crash? The key here is that very thing so conspicuously absent from the scene before the crash, namely, conviviality. Before the workman falls, each person in the room is sunk in himself, "bogged down" as Will puts it. The sudden crash wrests each from his isolation and unites him with the others by virtue of their mutual danger, surprise, and after a moment, relief at having escaped injury. It is this new-found conviviality which dispels the murk of noxious particles. Light and substance are restored to the world and both persons and paintings can suddenly be seen with new clarity.

Notice that as in the context of developing an alternative model of theory based upon storytelling, we find once again the concepts "clarity" and "conviviality" in close, friendly, and therefore unconventional proximity to one another. In this second appearance of the odd couple lies the heart of our parable. First, it is significant that the physical appearance of Barrett and the others is momentarily altered by a shower of fine glass:

> For there he was, the worker, laid out and powdered head to toe
> like a baker. Some seconds passed before the engineer realized
> that it was glass that turned him white, glass powdered to sugar.
> It covered the family too. They stood for an age gazing at each
> other, turned into pillars of salt; then, when they saw that no one
> was hurt, they fell into one another's arms, weeping and laughing.

This transformation, which we might expect to be a source of additional confusion, even fear, has in fact a strangely liberating effect, a paradox which must not pass unnoticed. To use St. Paul's image, it is as if before they saw through a glass darkly but now they see face to face (1 Corinthians 13:12). What does it mean in this context "to see face to face"? It does not mean here any more than in Corinthians to see with perfect lucidity and in the instant all the world arrayed before one. Moreover, it is conspicuously not the case that the clarity issues from the deliberate marshaling of clear and distinct ideas. On the contrary, that clarity is implicated or *folded into* the incident itself. Further, the simple fact that the stuff of the incident is an indecorous mix of the accidental, the destructive, and the life-threatening lends additional credence to the thesis that the clarity which obtains after the crash does not fit the Cartesian model. Instead, "to see face to face" is to know and value the concreteness and particularity of both self and other; it is to feel their fragility in the neighborhood of injury and death and to rejoice nonetheless. Most important, this new knowledge cannot be abstracted from the situation in which Barrett and the others find themselves. It is not a moveable feast. Rather, logically of a piece with the nature of truth itself, this knowledge is dramatic and agonistic and not to be had apart from a convivial setting.

In this connection, it is of no small significance that, for Will at least, the salubrious effect of this incident does not last. The next morning, solitary once again, he buys the telescope, convinced that the lenses "penetrated to the heart of things." Like Tom More of *Love in the Ruins,* with his Quantitative Qualitative Ontological Lapsometer, Will Barrett unwittingly and to his cost chooses his weapon from the arsenal of the enemy. In a way perfectly analogous to Martian-essayist-Percy's reliance upon the tokens of behaviorism in "The Delta Factor," the telescope just as surely blinds Will to the appropriate implications of his sense that he and his fellows are in deep trouble. Instead of true conviviality, it provides an artificial closeness in which people, no less than individual bricks in a far building, are reduced to the status of objects to be observed in a noncomittal way. Hence, as do Helen Keller, the liquid water, and the word *water* in Percy's "The Delta Factor" triangle, so do persons, bricks, and anything else within the telescope's range enjoy an equal ontological footing when viewed through the mechanical eye. Rather than "recovering things" as Will hopes, his fine instrument only pushes them farther away, making him more vulnerable than ever to attack by the ravening particles.

Thus is the episode in the art museum divided neatly in two by the workman's fall from the skylight. The reason why this is worth remarking at length should be clear when we consider the implications of the similarities between Will Barrett in this episode and Percy-as-Martian in "The Delta Factor." As we have seen, two importantly different models of theory and clarity are at work for Percy in the opening essay of *The Message in the Bottle.* Further, his use of the Cartesian model is decidedly infelicitous, while his use of a narrative model has much happier results. The case can now be made that the scene in the Metropolitan recapitulates in narrative terms the strengths and weaknesses, the sundry pretensions and intentions of Percy's argument in that essay—i.e., Will Barrett's ups and downs, his insight pitted against his penchant for detachment are the very embodiment of Percy's own profound intellectual ambivalence and confusion in "The Delta Factor."

How so? The onto-epistemic situation which obtains before the crash is logically of a piece with that which obtains when Percy takes up the conceptual tools of Cartesianism and launches a frontal assault on the regnant philosophical tradition of the West. Like Will, the harder he looks, the less he sees. To put it differently, the epistemology and ontology folded into this phenomenon is analogous to that implied in the phenomenon of writing a philosophical essay the aim of which is to dismantle the Cartesian picture of the self but in which the author relies upon the philosophical dispositions which uphold that picture. Just as the ravenous particles clog the air in the museum, cutting Will and the others off from one another, so do the analogies, metaphors, images, and rhetorical strategies that comprise the Cartesian framework come between Percy-as-essayist and his roots in the human world of actors and speakers.

In contrast, the onto-epistemic situation which obtains after the crash is logically homogenous with that which obtains for Percy when he puts his critique of modern culture into a story; or, in the case of "The Delta Factor," in the context of "little dramas" and linguistic tokens whose bent is toward the concrete, the active, and the incarnate. The way of knowing and being implied in the phenomenon of seeing persons and paintings clearly because one has been forcefully remanded to the concrete world in which death may come suddenly and in which the lived mind-body and the company of one's fellows are thereby made precious is analogous to that implied in the phenomenon of storytelling. The workman's fall renders the activity of *mere spectation* conspicuously inappropriate to the situation at hand; so too does the storyteller's language game render the regnant model of reflection inappropriate as a tool with which to think about the nature of man in the postmodern age. It provides instead an instrument much better suited to the task of thinking about a creature in which Word and Flesh struggle to become one.

I have suggested that the tension so evident in "The Delta Factor" between two radically different ways of thinking about man informs all of Percy's work. Here in this brief episode from *The Last Gentleman* we find that tension equally sharp. The important difference and the important point is that as the author of *The Last Gentleman* Percy is no less aware of Will Barrett's weaknesses and the inadequacy of his orientation to the world than he is of his singular gifts. By placing this particular character in a particular situation, he clearly and concretely illustrates the pernicious effects of even the most tacit acquiescence to the dicta of Cartesianism vis-à-vis the self. As the author of "The Delta Factor," however, he seems unaware of this proclivity in himself. More precisely, he is unaware of it when as the author of the second major part of "The Delta Factor" he abandons the pleasantly "unedifying" language game of the storyteller in favor of the decidedly edifying one of the closet behaviorist.

Thus this dense episode from Percy's second novel seems to bear out the thesis that Percy thinks most clearly when he uses the novel rather than the philosophical essay as his instrument for reflection. The implications of this scene are borne out in his first and third novels and in two essays from *The Message in the Bottle* as well. There we shall find that so long as he employs the tokens and follows the pretensions of the storyteller's language game, Percy is consistently successful at "getting around the ravenous particles"—i.e., at sustaining an attack upon the philosophic tradition of the West that is unerring in its accuracy and devastating in its potency.

Earlier, I observed that Will Barrett and Binx Bolling, protagonist of *The Moviegoer,* have at least one thing in common: they are both "onto something." What Binx is onto is "the search," and like Will's clairvoyance in the matter of ravenous particles, his clear sense of both the possibility and the necessity of embarking upon the search is our best clue as to how things stand with him. Just what the search is and how it is apposite to his predicament is the heart of the novel, and there we shall focus our attention. Specifically, I want to suggest that Binx's predicament is analogous to that of Will Barrett in the museum before the crash; his situation too bears the unmistakable mark of our culture's tacit and wholesale adherence to the Cartesian picture of the self. Further, like the workman's fall, the way out of that predicament implicated in "the search" brings together certain concepts judged logically heterogeneous according to the Cartesian framework. Like that of Barrett, Binx's predicament may thus be shown to reflect Percy's firm grasp of the conceptual issues at stake in a narrative critique of Cartesianism.

What exactly is Binx's predicament? There is nothing which immediately suggests itself as a source of difficulty. He is young, attractive, and intelligent. He has plenty of money and enjoys making it as a stockbroker. Unlike Will Barrett, he does not suffer from amnesia or any other peculiar ailments. He is fond of women and they of him. It is true that his father was afflicted with melancholy and died a rather too romantic death, drowned in the sea off Crete, a copy of *A Shropshire Lad* in his pocket. Binx finds this recollection troubling at times but is more often simply puzzled and bemused by his sense that it is somehow a clue in his search; exactly how and why is unclear.

In what way, then, might we say that Binx is a man in a predicament? First, like Barrett he knows that, the pleasantries of life notwithstanding, all is not well. More than once he refers to the spoiler as "the malaise": "What is the malaise? you ask. The malaise is the pain of loss. The world is lost to you, the world and the people in it, and there remains only you and the world and you no more able to be in the world than Banquo's ghost."

Consider carefully what Binx is saying here. The "ghost at a feast" image is one which we have seen Percy use in "The Delta Factor" to describe the plight of modern man exiled from the world, ironically, by the very science which has transformed that world for his benefit and comfort. As one who feels that exile keenly, Binx speaks right to the heart of the dilemma. Indeed, his definition of the malaise might equally be described as a concise statement of what it is like to live as though the Cartesian picture of the self upheld by modern science were exhaustively true; as though the "I" were synonymous with a discarnate mind reluctantly inhabiting an insensate body and loosed upon a world of equally insensate and hostile objects.

Binx's remark is particularly arresting not merely because it is succinct; its real potency lies in its *situatedness*. When he speaks of the loss of the world, his fellows, and consequently of himself, Binx does not do so as one who makes an abstract philosophical proposition which might be uttered by Anyone, Anyplace. Instead, he speaks as one man to another ("What is the malaise? *you ask*.") and as one who feels the pain of this loss on ordinary Wednesday mornings in old New Orleans. To put it simply, the sense of loss that haunts Binx cannot be abstracted from a particular person who finds himself in a particular predicament; it *cannot be* apart from Binx's story. So obvious that its significance might be overlooked, this fact is most important. By presenting us not with sweeping generalizations about modern culture or the nature of modern man but rather with one John Bickerson Bolling, a certain man who finds himself in a certain situation, Percy effectively stretches our minds and imaginations away from that habit of thought governed by the spirit of abstraction. As in the first pages of "The Delta Factor," he invites us instead to attend both *from* and *to* the particulars of persons in predicaments, our reflections pretended by the concrete tokens of the storyteller's language game.

Binx's economical response to the question "What is the malaise?" is neither the first nor the last time the long shadow of Descartes falls across his story. The loss of world, self, and other implicit in Cartesian thought makes itself felt at almost every turn. Three passages are especially telling in this regard. Two involve Binx alone while the third includes his cousin, Kate Cutrer, and each gives evidence of Percy's firm control over his conceptual territory.

Very early in the novel, Binx tells us something about his life—his family, his brokerage business, his domestic arrangements in the suburb of Gentilly, and the special pleasure he takes in going to movies. The only thing remarkable in all this is that Binx's life seems as unremarkable as the suburb in which he lives. Indeed, he sets great store by being so unexceptional; it is a trait he cultivates assiduously. Of particular interest in the present context is what by Binx's own estimation gives this quiet life shape and coherence:

> Life in Gentilly is very peaceful. . . . I am a model tenant and a model citizen and take pleasure in doing all that is expected of me. My wallet is full of identity cards, library cards, credit cards. . . . It is a pleasure to carry out the duties of a citizen and to receive in return a receipt or a neat styrene card with one's name on it certifying, so to speak, one's right to exist.

No less pointedly than do the images in "The Delta Factor" of sundry folk feeling good in bad environments and vice versa, Binx's self-portrait attests to the poverty of a picture of the self which divorces mind from body and denies both any purchase or status in the human world of speech and action. How so? In Binx's case the bankruptcy of such a picture is embodied quite vividly in his belief that his identity is contingent upon that most impersonal and featureless of modern inventions, the plastic credit card. Only by keeping a firm grip on his wallet full of cards and by "doing all that is expected of [him]," can Binx reassure himself that he does indeed exist. Thus for the present at least, when called upon to give an account of himself *as a self,* Binx does not do so in terms of speech and action. The tokens which do come to hand are abstracted from any plexus of words, deeds, and human relationships and are informed instead by one of the principle theses of Cartesian thought, namely, that mathematics is the measure of all things. The move from this notion to that which posits one's "right to exist" in numbers on a card (numbers which might equally be assigned to Anyone, Anyplace, Anytime) is neither far nor difficult.

Binx has been reduced to this unhappy state precisely because the potent though unobtrusive legacy of the Enlightenment is such that he is constrained to think of the self in just these terms at the exclusion of all others; most particularly, at the exclusion of any model or conceptual framework which acknowledges the fact of our embodiment. Later, recalling his reading habits before getting onto the search, Binx realizes the price of this exclusion:

> Until recent years, I read only "fundamental" books, that is, key books on key subjects. . . . During those years, I stood outside the universe and sought to understand it. I lived in my room as an Anyone living Anywhere and read fundamental books and only for diversion took walks around the neighborhood and saw an occasional movie. Certainly it did not matter to me where I was when I read such a book as *The Expanding Universe.* . . .

> The only difficulty was that though the universe had been disposed of, I myself was left over. There I lay in my hotel room with my search over yet still obliged to draw one breath and then the next.

The echo here of the charge Kierkegaard leveled against Hegel, namely, that he had built a large and beautiful structure in which to house everything in the universe save himself, who must live outside in a miserable hut, is unmistakable. It would not be overstating the case to say that Binx no less than Søren Kierkegaard has stumbled upon the best-kept secret of modern philosophy: If a man tries to live according to the precepts of that philosophy, he will inevitably find himself as homeless as Ishmael and a castaway twice over—first, cast out of Eden and condemned to know the pain of death and of God's silence; and then cast out of himself so that the personal pronoun "I" is emptied out, bereft of any habitation in the city of man. Thus is the world outside the garden equally lost to him. This is precisely the dilemma Binx embodies in the guise of "Anyone living Anywhere" with a pocketful of credit cards and reading "fundamental" books. The one question his books cannot answer is that which Percy, like Kierkegaard, keeps always in hand: What is it to be a man and to live and die?

The toll so quietly and relentlessly taken upon the human spirit by the struggle to live up to the demands of being Anyone, Anyplace is almost always before us in *The Moviegoer*. Perhaps nowhere in the novel is that toll so distressingly clear as near the end when Binx and Kate make love on the train going to Chicago. The relationship between these two is an important part of the novel and plays an important role in the progress of Binx's search. Being in a somewhat precarious mental state, Kate is especially vulnerable to the malaise. Always either falling behind herself or leaping ahead of herself, as Binx puts it, she never quite comes to rest, never quite coincides with herself. Consequently, she is rather like Tom More in *Love in the Ruins* and subject to night exaltations and morning terrors. For all of that, however, she is a most thoughtful and intelligent young woman who knows she is in a predicament. In this, she and Binx have much in common and so are drawn together.

At the novel's end, Kate and Binx are married. This commitment is possible, however, only after they have tasted together the bitter despair of knowing that "flesh poor flesh" cannot *of itself* rescue one from the numbing effects of the malaise:

> Flesh poor flesh failed us. The burden was too great and flesh poor flesh, neither hallowed by sacrament nor despised by spirit

(for despising is not the worst fate to overtake the flesh), but until this moment seen through and cancelled, rendered null by the cold and fishy eye of the malaise—flesh poor flesh now at this moment summoned all at once to be all and everything, end all and be all, the last and only hope—quails and fails. The truth is that I was frightened half to death by her bold (not really bold, not whorish bold but *theorish* bold) carrying on. . . . Kate too was scared. We shook like leaves. (Emphasis mine.)

The burden under which Binx and Kate labor does not issue from the absence of love and care. Their difficulty lies in being without a human habitation for that love and care. The discovery they make is that the flesh has been so thoroughly and systematically nullified by the logical dominance of mind in modern culture that the living body has become in effect exactly as Descartes said—not significantly different from the flesh of a corpse. It is a nothing, a zero, "mere flesh." As such, it is equally unfit as a vessel for love or hate but is simply empty. Consequently, like those scientists in *Love in the Ruins* who are utterly abstracted from the ordinary world and seek to reenter it by engaging in the most bestial behavior, so do Binx and Kate demand too much of "flesh poor flesh" and likewise fail.

As painful as it is, however, their failure is neither final nor complete because they have the advantage of knowing themselves to be in a predicament. The clue to the resolution of that predicament evident in their eventual marriage lies in the nature of the search. And what is that exactly. Binx has this to say:

> The search is what anyone would undertake if he were not sunk in the everydayness of his own life. This morning, for example, I felt as if I had come to myself on a strange island. And what does such a castaway do? Why, he pokes around the neighborhood and doesn't miss a trick.
>
> To become aware of the possibility of the search is to be onto something. Not to be onto something is to be in despair.

The notion of "coming to oneself" and the image of the castaway turn up often in Percy's writing and do important work in each instance. Usually the former occurs as a result of some disaster which shakes one loose from the grip of "everydayness." Binx, we learn, came to himself lying on the ground under a chindolea bush in Korea in 1951, seriously wounded in the shoulder. What should have been a very bad time for him was, in typical Percian inside-out fashion, a very good one. Why? It was good because all that had been lost to him in the malaise was momentarily recovered, and for a brief time everything was imbued with an astonishing substance and reality. Like the paintings in the Metropolitan after the crash, things could be seen. Binx goes on to say, "As I watched, there awoke in me an immense curiosity. I was onto something. I vowed that if I ever got out of this fix, I would pursue the search." Binx can never say precisely what is the object of his search and is always on the lookout for clues—e.g., his father, the Jews, movies. Moreover, for long stretches he loses entirely his sense of being "onto something" but sooner or later it returns to him, always unexpected and usually prompted by his being suddenly struck with the splendid presence and concreteness of some person or object or scene.

The other important notion here is implicit in the image of the castaway. The particular sort of castaway Binx had in mind here is not the one who "comes to himself in a strange place . . . and settles down with a vengeance. In two weeks time, he is so sunk in everydayness that he might just as well be dead." Rather Binx's castaway is a seeker who, to borrow an image from "The Message in the Bottle," never forgets he is not at home and awaits the newsbearer who can tell him who he is and where home is. An important part of being onto something and so avoiding the worst sort of despair is just this awareness. It is to know that one's self is not equivalent to the sum of the particulars of one's everyday life.

This image of the castaway, together with the notion of coming to oneself, suggests that at stake in the search is nothing less than the acknowledgment and acceptance of that tension between immanence and transcendence which makes us what we humanly are as selves. When Binx "comes to himself" under the chindolea bush, the world that had been lost to him, including his own body, is given back in all its concreteness, in all its unyielding immanence. At the same moment, however, he is filled with, as he says, "an immense curiosity" and becomes henceforth "a seeker." The world recovered, Binx knows himself to be very much in the world and rejoices in its and his concrete reality. Yet he also knows himself not to be exhaustively defined by that world; he is a castaway the secret of whose identity is held by one across the sea.

Whereas flesh, poor flesh must fail Kate and Binx when they demand that it be the repository *simpliciter* of their respective selves, to acknowledge that same flesh as the necessary ground of but not equivalent to "an Otherness that can say 'I'" (W. H. Auden, *For the Time Being*) is to be onto something very precious indeed. Thus Binx's search promises to be a fine antidote to the malaise. But does what we learn in the epilogue seem to bear out this hope? Given his marriage to Kate, his plans to go to medical school, etc., we might think that Binx gives up the search and succumbs to that very everydayness he so wishes to avoid. Percy himself suggests another interpretation, however, when he says that, in Kierkegaardian terms, Binx "jumps from the aesthetic mode clear across the ethical to the religious. He has no ethical sphere at all." This remark seems quite appropriate to Binx's situation when we remember that in Kierkegaard's account of the Abraham and Isaac story Abraham returns from Mount Moriah and says nothing to Sarah of his experience. Instead, he goes quietly about his business looking and speaking like the most ordinary tax collector. The knight of faith is always so disguised: "Those . . . who carry the jewel of faith are likely to be delusive because their outward appearance bears a striking resemblance to that which both the infinite resignation and faith profoundly despise . . . to Philistinism." In this improbable knight, the immanent and the transcendent come together with a serenity that is not empty and perilous like that of Will Barrett's fellow museum goers. Rather, his is a serenity born of the redemption of the mundane world achieved, paradoxically, by his first giving it up and then believing past all reckoning that he will be given it back again. Simply put, the knight of faith rejoices in the beauty of his island even as he discovers himself to be a castaway who can never be fully at home on that island.

One more point needs to be made about Kierkegaard's knight of faith, and it is most important. In Kierkegaard's view, that which makes Abraham the knight of faith is not contemplation but action. Further, the test to which God puts him is no test apart from the value placed upon the temporal and mundane love of father for son and the promise of descendants "countless as the dust of the earth" (Genesis 13:16). Faith, then, is not a moveable feast, for it has no meaning, no habitation apart from the terrible predicament of one man. It is rather profoundly *situated* in the world, in the lived mindbody. There and only there may the transcendent, nonspecifiable "I" appear. Thus does Kierkegaard redeem the self from both the limits of "flesh poor flesh" and the homelessness of disembodied mind.

Now in the case of Binx, we do not, of course, have such a dramatic test of faith as God's command to Abraham that he sacrifice Isaac. Even so, the Binx of the novel's close has undergone some subtle and important changes which indicate that he has made the movement of faith. For instance, his secretary-chasing days over, his and Kate's "frail enterprise in love" has matured into marriage. Aunt Emily has admitted that he is "not one of her heroes but a very ordinary fellow'; consequently, they get along much better than before. When his fifteen-year-old half brother dies of a massive infection, Binx answers truthfully when asked by the other children if Lonnie is going to die. He also answers their other and perhaps more difficult questions with compassion and without the slightest hesitation:

> "Binx ... when our Lord raises us up on the last day, will Lonnie still be in a wheelchair or will he be like us?"
> "He'll be like you."
> "You mean he'll be able to ski?" The children cock their heads and listen like old men.
> "Yes."

Perhaps most telling, he has only this to say about his search:

> As for my search, I have not the inclination to say much on the subject. For one thing, I have not the authority as the great Danish philosopher declared, to speak of such matters in any way other than the edifying. For another thing, it is not open to me even to be edifying, since the time is later than his, much too late to edify or do much of anything except plant a foot in the right place as the opportunity presents itself—if indeed asskicking is properly distinguished from edification.

Typical of the knight of faith, Binx declines to assume the responsibility of one who speaks with authority. That position properly belongs to the apostle or the newsbearer. Instead, he is content to go quietly along his way merely engaging now and then in some helpful asskicking.

In a word, all that was restless and at times a little manic in Binx has disappeared, to be replaced by a sense of quiet assurance, the assurance of a man at home with the world and with himself. This quiet is not, however, that of dumb passivity. Rather, it is that of a man who stands ready to hear the newsbearer whenever and wherever he appears; of one no longer torn between his island home and his home across the sea but who waits and watches patiently, confident that the news will come one day. Moreover, the faith signified by this posture is not one which permits Binx to follow the example of St. Anthony and withdraw to the desert to await the Lord's coming. Rather, he is called to work in the vineyard, loving, nurturing, and supporting Kate, Aunt Emily, his half brothers and sisters. As he thinks to himself when Kate asks what he plans to do:

> There is only one thing I can do: listen to people, see how they stick themselves into the world, hand them along a ways on their dark journey and be handed along. And for good and selfish reasons. It only remains to decide whether this vocation is best pursued in a service station or—

As it happens, Binx chooses medical school over the attractive alternative of running a small service station, but the important point is that what he clearly perceives to be his vocation carries him out into the world to "hand people along" and be handed along in turn. It is this—not reading fundamental books, not living as Anyone, Anyplace, not endlessly going to movies—but this care and conviviality for and with the living creature, mortal, guilty, beautiful, which defeats the malaise. Perhaps too this is what it is to be a man and to live and die.

As in *The Last Gentleman*, Percy's modus operandi in *The Moviegoer* is to present us with a person in a predicament. Also as in *The Last Gentleman*, that predicament is closely tied to the influence upon our culture of a certain picture of the self implicit in the dominant philosophic tradition of the West. Thus Percy chooses for himself as author and for us as readers a certain framework and certain conceptual tools with which to consider the efficacy of that picture. The ensuing critique is both conceptually clear and polemically on target, demonstrating once again the acuity of his insight into the whys and wherefores of man's terrible unhappiness in the twentieth century. Too it lends further support to my thesis that as an instrument for reflection, storytelling is superior to abstract philosophical argument when it comes to thinking about and perhaps even alleviating that unhappiness. *Love in the Ruins* will provide even more support for both these points.

The fine wit and sense of irony evident in both *The Moviegoer* and *The Last Gentleman* together with the singular liberties available to the satirist make *Love in the Ruins* a wickedly funny and polemically devastating novel. In the story of Thomas More, M.D., widower, psychiatrist, alcoholic, and self-proclaimed bad Catholic (but a believer nonetheless), Percy takes deadly aim at the more conspicuous insanities of "the Christ-forgetting, Christ-haunted death-dealing Western world." Almost no one escapes his satiric reach: liberals, conservatives, blacks, whites, Roman Catholics, Protestants—just to name a few—are equally chastised for their complicity in the imminent demise of Western culture.

At the heart of that demise is what Tom More is pleased to call "More's syndrome, or: chronic angelism-bestialism that rives soul from body and sets it orbiting the great world as the spirit of abstraction whence it takes the form of beasts, swans and bulls, werewolves, bloodsuckers, Mr. Hydes, or just poor lonesome ghost locked in its own machinery." Thanks to Percy's judicious use of the satirist's license for hyperbole, it is at once amusingly and painfully clear that this "chronic-angelism-bestialism" riddles the novel's private and public worlds and that it sets every man equally against his neighbor and himself, diagnostician More no less than the others. It is in this world that Thomas More, M.D., distant kinsman of Sir Thomas More ("Why can't I follow More's example, love myself less, God and my fellow man more, and leave whiskey and women alone?") bravely and not too humbly ("I am . . . nevertheless a genius . . . who sees into the hidden causes of things and erects simple hypotheses to account for the glut of everyday events.") sets out to "weld the broken self whole." The tool with which he hopes to accomplish this feat is an unprepossessing little gadget dubbed "More's Quantitative Qualitative Ontological Lapsometer." "With it," he claims, "any doctor can probe the very secrets of the soul, diagnose the maladies that poison the wellsprings of man's hope. It could save the world or destroy it."

Tom More and his invention are the center of the novel. What is of particular interest in the present context is the discrepancy between his skills as a diagnostician and his skill at effecting a cure. This discrepancy is not merely a matter of, having once made a diagnosis, being uncertain as to the correct prescription. Rather, it reflects a profound confusion analogous to that evident in Percy himself in "The Delta Factor." Having made an astute diagnosis of certain peculiarly modern maladies afflicting body and spirit alike, More is then seduced by modern science, in the rather scruffy guise of one Art Immelman, into believing that if we just had the right machine and could tinker with the right brain cells, all could be made well. As we have seen in "The Delta Factor," this is rather like setting the fox to guard the henhouse, and More's enterprise meets with about as much success. The important point, however, is that, as we have seen in the predicament of Will Barrett and Binx Bolling, Percy is well aware of More's weakness and confusion and is, by implication, fully in control of his material.

The extent to which this is the case is particularly clear in the doctor's dealings with Immelman. Looking like "the sort of fellow who used to service condom vendors in the old Auto Age," Art plays an appropriately deadbeat Mephistopheles to More's alcoholic Faust. Percy once remarked, "The great difference between Dr. More and the other heroes is that Dr. More has no philosophical problems. He knows what he believes." He might have added that More also knows what he likes and in what order: "I believe in God and the whole business but I love women best, music and science next, whiskey next, God fourth, and my fellow man hardly at all. Generally I do as I please." It is to this hierarchy that Art appeals when he offers More the one thing he cannot resist, the power to know and love and to win at both. Significantly, "to know" means here to know abstractly; "to love" means to love not a particular woman but all women. As Art puts it:

You stimulate the scientist-lover . . . so that in the same moment

one becomes victorious in science one also becomes victorious in
love. And all for the good of mankind! Science to help all men
and a happy joyous love to help all women. . . . This love has its
counterpart in scientific knowledge: it is neutral morally, abstractive and godlike . . . in the sense of being like a god in one's
freedom and omniscience.

The prospect of becoming Faust and Don Juan all at once is too much for
More to resist. But how is the shaky doctor to be so transformed, and what
is the price? We all know the devil gives away nothing for free.

The answer lies in More's invention. An experienced encephalographer,
he has a hunch that with a wireless gadget similar to an encephalograph he
might be able to measure electrical activity in specific areas of the brain.
With a little help from a colleague, he puts just such a machine together.
The problem remaining is this: "Given such a machine, given such readings,
could the readings then be correlated with the manifold woes of the Western
world, its terrors and rages and murderous impulses? And if so, could the
latter be treated by treating the former?" More believes the answer is yes if
only the right "dosage" could be found.

Eventually Tom succeeds in correlating certain patterns of electrical activity in the brain with various manifestations of chronic angelism-bestialism.
Until Art comes along, however, his lapsometer is useful only as a diagnostic
tool and not as a therapeutic one. The curious Mr. Immelman, who speaks
the worst sort of bureaucratic jargon and always appears and disappears
under the most peculiar circumstances, has the answer: an attachment which
will enable More to alter these electrical patterns and effect at least a tem-
porary cure for, say, night exaltation, morning terror, conservative fits, radical seizures, and abstracted lust, not to mention large-bowel complaints. In
short, he offers More the alleged means by which to cure the very soul of
Western man, healing the rift between mind and body by which he was cast
out of himself. As if this prospect were not seductive enough, More is also
assured, Art tells him, of winning a Nobel Prize. Since he is as vain as he is
well-meaning, this last helps him to overcome his vague distrust of Immelman. In return, all he has to do is hand over to Art all his lapsometers plus
patent rights.

What is the issue here? The key is "*alleged* means of cure." In the same
interview in which Percy commented on More's lack of philosophical problems, he also said this: "The big mistake was in him, that he could believe
he could treat a spiritual disease with a scientific device however sophisticated." What More proposes to do with his lapsometer is to fight fire with

fire using the conceptual tools of science to compensate for the inadequacies of science. What Percy proposes to do in his "The Delta Factor" triangle is, remember, logically analogous—merely to "improve" upon an old therapy, an old way of thinking about the human creature rather than to develop a radically new therapy and so avoid the conceptual traps so well hidden in the old. The important point is that once again we find that Percy-as-storyteller, in contrast to Percy-as-essayist, is onto the fallacy of this approach.

The evidence that this is so is not confined to a single remark in a single interview. The most substantial proof is in the novel itself. Not only does More's invention exacerbate rather than cure the symptoms of "More's syndrome" and with disastrous results; there is in addition one character who intimates the radical therapy which is the appropriate antidote to chronic angelism-bestialism and which More fails to effect with his invention. The character is Father Smith, priest to the small remnant of a once large Roman Catholic congregation.

Father Smith appears at several important points in the novel. Like More and unlike any other character, he knows that times are very bad and that man is in deep trouble. He does not, however, talk about "chronic angelism-bestialism"; rather he says, "The channels are jammed and the word is not getting through. . . . The news [is] being jammed . . . principalities and powers have won and we've lost . . . death is winning, life is losing." Obviously, Father Smith is feeling rather low and his response to this dismal situation is significantly different from More's. Central to the priest's assessment of his and his fellows' predicament is "news"—not brain waves, not heavy sodium and chloride ions, but "news." As we have seen in "The Delta Factor" and shall see again in "The Message in the Bottle," the notion of news is at the heart of what Percy takes to be a coherent theory of man. Moreover, it is "the clue and sign" of man's salvation. That it should turn up here in just this context is most important. Implicit in the priest's suggestion is a conceptual framework which is logically at odds with the scientific and tacitly Cartesian one of More. It is a measure of the latter's obtuseness on this point that, knowing Smith operates a ham radio, Tom dismisses his remark as merely a lapse into ham radio jargon. For his part, the priest does not straighten him out by making his framework explicit. Instead, he simply goes on about his business, hearing confessions, saying the Mass, baptizing the newborn, and burying the dead.

By thus linking news or the lack of it with the unhappy state of affairs he sees around him, the otherwise unremarkable Father Smith makes an important conceptual move which More, constrained as he is by the con-

ceptual framework of science, cannot make. In effect, the priest quietly introduces into the chaos of More's world the possibility of welding the broken
self whole by means of an instrument which cannot be manufactured, as can
the lapsometer, in an Osaka computer plant. Father Smith's instrument is
not a moveable feast. Rather, it is folded into his own speech and action and
into the news of which he is the bearer. Further, if the word gets through at
all, it will be only to one who knows himself to be in a certain predicament
and so stands in the way of hearing news.

Soon after this scene, Father Smith disappears, to reappear only in the
epilogue, set at Christmas Eve five years after the main action of the novel.
In the interim, society has been burned inside out with the "Bantus" now
occupying the top of the economic and social ladder and the white folks the
bottom. Not much has really changed, however. The Bantus now suffer night
exaltations and morning terrors just like the white man. The local scientists
are more abstracted from themselves than ever. The broken self is, in a word,
still broken. But two things have changed. First Art Immelman is gone,
dispatched by a desperate prayer offered up by Tom More to his kinsman:
"Sir Thomas More, kinsman, saint, best, dearest, merriest of Englishmen,
pray for us and drive this son of a bitch hence." Second, the latter-day More
has given up both Early Times and vodka-Tang-duck-egg breakfasts, married
Ellen, his rather tart Presbyterian nurse, fathered two children, and makes
a very modest living as a physician. He does continue to tinker with his
invention and has not quite given up hope that one day he will be able to
cure as well as diagnose chronic angelism-bestialism.

An economical way to describe this change in More is to say that he
now stands in the way of hearing news. This is not to claim that he has
resolved all his difficulties. On the contrary, he frequently yearns for a drink
and admits that mornings are "still not the best of times." Even so, More
no longer aspires to be either Faust or Don Juan but has settled into a middle
place inhabited by neither angels nor beasts:

> Strange: I am older, yet there seems to be more time, time for
> watching and thinking and working. I am a poor man but a
> kingly one. If you want and wait and work, you can have. . . .
> What I want is no longer the Nobel, screw prizes, but just to
> figure out what I've hit upon. Someday, a man will walk into my
> office as ghost or beast or ghost-beast and walk out as a man,
> which is to say sovereign wanderer, lordly exile, worker, and
> waiter, and watcher.

In short, More lives in the world in a way quite different from before. Even his lingering aspiration to do that which he probably cannot do reflects this change from Faust/Don Juan to wayfarer/castaway. To go from the lust to know and love abstractly to the relatively modest business of figuring out what one has "hit upon" and using that discovery to heal is to make an important change indeed. It is one which anchors More and his invention in the mundane and concrete world of actors and speakers.

Pride is tenacious, however, and More is far from being rid of it. When after a hiatus of eleven years he goes to confession on Christmas Eve, he is angry and disappointed when Father Smith seems unimpressed, even bored, with his catalog of sins and, more important, with the fact that he is not particularly sorry to have committed them. What Smith realizes and More does not is that such sins as Tom's are but a distraction from the more serious ills of the human spirit, which are also more banal. He tells More:

> Meanwhile, forgive me but there are other things we must think about: like doing our jobs, you being a better doctor, I being a better priest, showing a bit of ordinary kindness to people, particularly in our own families—unkindness to those close to us is a pitiful thing—doing what we can for our poor unhappy country—things which, please forgive me, sometimes seem more important than dwelling on a few middle-aged day-dreams.

More finally understands:

> "You're right, I'm sorry," I say instantly, scalded.
> "You're sorry for your sins?"
> "Yes. Ashamed rather."
> "That will do . . . go in peace."

More does go in peace, humbled when reminded by Father Smith of Jesus' teaching that the first two commandments are greater than all the rest.

Love in the Ruins ends on this note of profound reconciliation. Like Binx Bolling, Tom More has learned to watch and wait and listen even as he rejoices in his wife, his children, and other earthly delights. In his story and most especially in the spectacular failure of More's Quantitative Qualitative Ontological Lapsometer, Percy again exposes the pernicious influence upon our culture and ourselves of the great Cartesian divide. The clarity and potency of his critique further attest to the great heuristic power of the conceptual tools at the storyteller's disposal.

Percy uses these tools with equal effectiveness in two essays from *The Message in the Bottle*, "The Loss of the Creature" and "Notes for a Novel About the End of the World." As different as they are in their particulars, these two essays have in common one characteristic which is very much to the point of my argument. In each, Percy's rhetorical strategy is to "anchor" his argument in one or more images of persons in predicaments. Reminiscent of his strategy in the first half of "The Delta Factor," this mode of argument is equally successful in these essays. Also as in "The Delta Factor" and in his first three novels, Percy's telos is to call our attention to the existential fallout precipitated by an allegiance to the Cartesian picture of the self. Once more, "little dramas of ordinary experience" are essential to the achievement of that end.

"The Loss of the Creature" opens with a reference to García López de Cárdenas, discoverer of the Grand Canyon. Percy soon discloses the nature of his interest in de Cárdenas when he observes, "Later the government set the place aside as a national park, hoping to pass along to millions the experience of Cárdenas. Does not one see the same sight from the Bright Angel Lodge that Cárdenas saw?" The answer in Percy's view is probably not. Why?

> The thing is no longer the thing as it confronted the Spaniard; it is rather that which has already been formulated—by picture postcard, geography book, tourist folders, and the words *Grand Canyon*. As a result of this preformulation, the source of the sightseer's pleasure undergoes a shift. Where the wonder and delight of the Spaniard arose from his penetration of the thing itself . . . now the sightseer measures his satisfaction *by the degree to which the canyon conforms to the preformed complex.* . . . The highest point, the term of the sightseer's satisfaction, is not the sovereign discovery of the thing before him; it is rather the measuring up of the thing to the criterion of the preformed symbolic complex.

Analogous to the loss which Binx speaks of in defining the malaise, this loss of sovereignty and the ontological and epistemological "shift" it embodies is the focus of Percy's attention in "The Loss of the Creature." His thesis is that this radical loss is a "consequence of the seduction of the layman by science," most conspicuous in "the caste of layman-expert," in which the layman is incapable of knowing or experiencing anything without the approving stamp of the expert. The result, he argues, is a twofold deprivation. First, the thing itself (e.g., Grand Canyon, Indian corn dance, Shakespearean sonnet) is devalued because it is so tidily "packaged." Second, the individual is himself devalued insofar as he assumes the role "not of the person but of the consumer."

Percy develops his argument around three images of persons in predicaments. The first I have already mentioned. The second is of a midwestern couple who stumble upon a remote Mexican village and witness a traditional religious festival. Their delight in this discovery, however, is contaminated by a certain uneasiness dispersed only when they return later with an ethnologist friend who can "certify their experience as genuine. . . . What they want from him is not ethnological explanations; all they want is his approval." The third predicament is that of a Scarsdale High biology student and a Sarah Lawrence English major, respectively, confronted by a dogfish and a Shakespearean sonnet. Fish and poem are "obscured" by the "educational package" in which they are presented. In each case, the student is hardpressed indeed to wrest them from these packages so that they may become something more than a mere specimen of sonnet or of dogfish; so that like the paintings in the Metropolitan, they may be seen.

Implicit in each of these scenarios are some of the same ontological and epistemological issues we have found elsewhere in Percy's work. Of special importance here is the connection he draws between the peculiar "placement" of these individuals in the world and the superordinance in our culture of theory over experience ("Placement" is Percy's word and he uses it in this connection at several important junctures in his argument, a point worth remarking given the importance of the notion of "placement" in *The Last Gentleman* and in the etymology of the word *epistemology*). The particulars of each little drama suggest that the model of theory Percy has in mind is the regnant one. In each instance, an individual conspires in his own disenfranchisement, his own demotion, so to speak, from person to consumer. This conspiracy would not be logically possible apart from an allegiance to an account of knowing governed by the spirit of abstraction, an account which, moreover, posits reality as atemporal and independent of any person. It is this concept of reality which constitutes the logical basis of the regnant model of theory.

The decisive factor in Percy's argument in "The Loss of the Creature" is that his reflections cannot be pried loose from their grounding in the concrete tokens of sightseeing, high school biology classes, and the like. At every point, he attends both *from* and *to* persons in predicaments. What he discloses in the process is that when one does otherwise—when, for example, one attends to a theory about individuals instead of to individuals themselves—a profound shift occurs in one's "placement" in the world. As Percy says at one point:

> The dogfish . . . [is] rendered invisible by a shift of reality from

concrete thing to theory which Whitehead has called the fallacy
of misplaced concreteness. It is the mistaking of an idea, a principle, an abstraction for the real. As a consequence of the shift,
the "specimen" is seen as less real than the theory of the specimen. As Kierkegaard said, once a person is seen as a specimen
of a race or a species, at that very moment he ceases to be
an individual. Then there are no more individuals but only
specimens.

The superordinance of the theoretical over the concrete Percy describes here
is precisely that epistemological situation which obtains in certain of his own
essays. In them, the consequence is the same, namely, the creature, the embodied self, disappears to be replaced by the *Cogito* and the abstract tokens
of Anyone, Anyplace. Yet in "The Loss of the Creature" he avoids that
conceptual trap by keeping his eye firmly fixed upon persons in predicaments.

Thus once again we find that Percy's own "placement" in the world vis-
à-vis his subject is contingent upon certain linguistic tokens whose bent is
in this instance undeniably toward the concrete, the active, and the incarnate.
As in the novels, that placement is such that he is at once constrained and
empowered to expose the logical inconsistencies implicit in the dictum *Cogito, ergo sum*. In contrast, one whose placement is on the side of that dictum,
so to speak, would not have at hand the conceptual tools with which to
discover that therein is the creature irretrievably lost; or if by chance he did
make such a discovery, it would be to him a matter of no philosophical
importance.

The most complex and striking image of a person in a predicament in
"Notes for a Novel About the End of the World" comes relatively late in
the essay. It is the image of a scientist-technician living in the near future,
by which time men have been divided into two classes, the consumer and
"the stranded objectivized consciousness, a ghost of a man who wanders the
earth like Ishmael." Our scientist is one of the latter. Percy goes on to characterize him in such a way as to make it clear that he has equally well in
hand here those epistemological and ontological issues so evident in the
novels and "The Loss of the Creature":

> Unlike the consumer he knows his predicament. He is the de-
> spairing man Kierkegaard spoke of, for whom there is hope be-
> cause he is aware of his despair. He is a caricature of the
> contemporary Cartesian man who has objectified the world and
> his body and sets himself over against both like the angel at the
> gates of Paradise. All creaturely relations crumble at his touch.

He has but to utter a word—*achieving intersubjectivity, inter-personal relations, meaningful behavior*—and that which the word signifies vanishes.

It would seem that this unfortunate scientist has been attacked by a veritable host of ravening particles. What will help him out of this predicament? The answer is consistent with the resolutions of both *The Moviegoer* and *Love in the Ruins*, namely, the Good News spoken with authority by a newsbearer, news which will prove apposite to the situation of him who stands in the way of hearing it.

This little drama is the centerpiece of "Notes for a Novel About the End of the World," an appropriate work with which to conclude this chapter on Percy as storyteller. In it, he reflects upon the vocation of the novelist and in particular upon that of the novelist who "has an explicit and ultimate concern with the nature of man and the nature of reality where man finds himself." Such a writer, he suggests, might rightly be called a "religious" novelist. Percy uses the word *religious* here in its root sense—i.e., as "signifying a radical bond as the writer sees it which connects man with reality—or the failure of such a bond—and so confers meaning to his life—or the absence of meaning." Of special concern to Percy is the function such a writer serves in modern, secular culture. At one point, he describes this function as "quasi-prophetic" and compares the novelist to a canary in a mine shaft: "The novelist is less like a prophet than he is like the canary that coal miners used to take down into the shaft to test the air. When the canary gets unhappy, utters plaintive cries, and collapses, it may be time for the miners to surface and think things over." As this splendid simile delivered in a typically sardonic tone suggests, Percy would concur with the thesis that the novelist possesses a kind of insight which distinguishes him from his fellows and issues in a singular clarity vis-à-vis the ills of modern culture. Indeed, his primary aim in this essay is to explore the nature and source of that clarity especially as it is evident in the religious novelist. Of special interest in the present context is the implication in Percy's argument that novelists *think* in a way importantly different from the way a scientist or a sociologist thinks. This point will be the focus of my discussion.

Percy opens this essay by characterizing the novelist's placement in the world in a way which must remind us of his "The Delta Factor" Martian:

Not being called by God to be a prophet, he nevertheless pretends to a certain prescience. If he did not think he saw something other people didn't see or at least didn't pay much attention to, he would be wasting his time writing and they reading. This does not mean that he is wiser than they. Rather it might testify to a species of affliction which sets him apart and gives him an odd point of view.

Like the Martian, the novelist stands apart from other men and can, therefore, see things to which they are blind. Throughout the essay Percy reiterates this point, emphasizing again and again the "oddness" of such a writer's perspective on men and society. What is significant about this Martian-novelist analogy is that here, no less than in "The Delta Factor," Percy treads a fine line between what I have characterized as appropriate versus inappropriate detachment from actors and speakers. In "The Delta Factor," as we have seen, he finally steps over the line onto the side of the latter. In "Notes for a Novel About the End of the World," however, he does not. Instead, as in his presentation of Will Barrett's unhappy aloofness, Percy is not seduced by the cult of objectivity. What seems to prevent such a capitulation is his explicit reliance upon the "incarnational, historical, and predicamental" world view of Judeo-Christianity, especially insofar as he employs this view as a framework according to which he may give an account of himself as a novelist. Thus are his reflections pretended by the tokens of that very story which, he argues in "The Delta Factor," comprises the only coherent theory of man. The result is that Percy displays an extraordinary insight into the singular powers of the novelist to countermand the "schism of consciousness" which afflicts modern, Western culture.

Two passages which follow closely upon one another in the text will serve to illustrate my point. First, the crux of Percy's argument is that the novelist's "categories" are importantly different from those of either the scientist or the sociologist. How so?

> If the scientist's vocation is to clarify and simplify, it would seem that the novelist's aim is to muddy and complicate. For he knows that even the most carefully contrived questionnaire cannot discover how it really stands with the sociologist or himself. What will be left out of even the most rigorous scientific formulation is nothing else than the individual himself. And since the novelist deals first and last with individuals and the scientist treats individuals only to discover their general properties, it is the novelist's responsibility to be chary of categories and rather to focus upon the mystery, the paradox, the *openness* of an individual human existence.

Implicated in this passage is the clear realization that, no matter how rigorous its application, the conceptual framework of science cannot exhaustively "accommodate" that perplexing mix of the transcendent and the immanent that is the embodied self. It cannot disclose to us what it is to be a man and to live and die.

Further—and with this, Percy puts his finger right on the heart of the matter—he also recognizes for what it is the great trap into which Tom More falls:

> For what has happened . . . is the absorption by the layman not of the scientific method but rather of the magical aura of science, whose credentials he accepts for all sectors of reality. Thus in the lay culture of a scientific society nothing is easier than to fall prey to a kind of seduction which sunders one's very self from itself into an all-transcending "objective" consciousness and a consumer-self with a list of "needs" to be satisfied. It is this monstrous bifurcation of man into angelic and bestial components against which old theologies must be weighed before new theologies are erected.

The "old theology" Percy has in mind is, as I have already indicated, that of the Judeo-Christian tradition in which man is neither angel nor beast but sovereign wayfarer; in which the world is consecrated as the locus of faith and of each man's responsibility to God and to other men. In comparison, Percy finds the new theologies to be "small potatoes indeed" and allows as how "to the 'religious' novelist, whether it be Sartre or O'Connor, the positive proposals of the new theology must sound like a set of resolutions passed by the P.T.A." It is this allegiance to the Christian story of birth, death, and resurrection, and to the Hebrew one of covenant, obligation, and God's speech, together with an unflagging focus upon persons in predicaments, which serves to anchor his reflections in the human world of word and deed. The result is a lively essay in which he takes a long and very thoughtful look at the vocation of the religious novelist. Consequently, we have an excellent opportunity to "hear" a superb storyteller reflecting upon the intricacies of his craft. What he has to say suggests that so long as he intends upon that craft, so long as he "thinks novelistically," his understanding of the human creature is very rich and fraught with the possibility of further discovery.

To claim that the three novels and two essays discussed here are significantly clearer and more polemically powerful than certain other of Percy's essays is not to claim that they embody a kind of perfect lucidity in the regnant, philosophical sense of that word. Nor is it to claim that the clarity of the novels and allied essays is merely a matter of their more readily yielding up certain themes or "ideas" which might be translated without loss of potency into the austere and putatively impersonal rhetoric of abstract, philosophical argument. Indeed, to make these claims would be to weaken rather than to strengthen my argument. Rather, the claim I do make is that the clarity and potency of these stories and essays is inextricably bound up with the metaphors, analogies, and rhetorical strategies which are the tools of the storyteller. That clarity and potency cannot be apart from their embodiment in the stuff of story whether that "stuff" be in a novel per se or woven into the imagery of a given essay. In both cases, the intent is the same, namely, to disclose the ills, the contradictions, the joys, and the sorrows of the human creature where and as we actually suffer them, in mind and heart, in body and spirit together; and in that compassionate disclosure, to comfort, to heal, and to rejoice.

As storyteller, Percy possesses insight into the rigors of the human condition which is informed by humor, compassion, and love. These three have no habitation apart from the mortal world. It is here and only here that the question "What does it mean to be a man and to live and die?" may be asked with any hope of an answer. It is this hope which Percy, unwittingly and to our mutual cost, surrenders when he turns to that austere and "rigorous" presentation of reality which is the highly abstract philosophical essay. In these essays ... the creature so splendidly present in the novels is truly lost.

Chronology

1916	Walker Percy born on May 28 in Birmingham, Alabama.
1917	Brother Leroy born.
1922	Brother Phinizy born.
1927	Percy's father, Leroy Percy, commits suicide.
1931	Percy's mother dies in automobile accident. Percy is adopted by his great uncle, William Alexander Percy, and moves to Greenville, Mississippi.
1937	Percy graduates from University of North Carolina and enrolls in medical school at Columbia College of Physicians and Surgeons.
1941	Percy receives his medical degree.
1942	Begins residency at Bellevue Hospital, New York City. Death of William Alexander Percy. Percy contracts tuberculosis.
1946	Marriage to Mary Bernice Townsend.
1947	Conversion to Roman Catholicism.
1948	Percy moves from New Orleans to Covington, Louisiana.
1954	Essay "Symbol as Need" is published in *Thought*.
1961	*The Moviegoer*.
1962	Receives National Book Award for *The Moviegoer*.
1966	*The Last Gentleman* nominated for National Book Award.
1971	*Love in the Ruins*.

1975   *The Message in the Bottle: How Queer Man Is, How Queer Language Is, and What One Has To Do With the Other.*

1977   *Lancelot.*

1980   *The Second Coming.*

1983   *Lost in the Cosmos: The Last Self-Help Book.*

Contributors

HAROLD BLOOM, Sterling Professor of the Humanities at Yale University, is the author of *The Anxiety of Influence, Poetry and Repression,* and many other volumes of literary criticism. His forthcoming study, *Freud: Transference and Authority,* attempts a full-scale reading of all of Freud's major writings. A MacArthur Prize Fellow, he is general editor of five series of literary criticism published by Chelsea House.

TONY TANNER is a Fellow of King's College, Cambridge, and the author of *The Reign of Wonder: Naivety and Reality in American Literature,* and *City of Words: American Fiction 1950–1970,* as well as studies of Conrad, Bellow, and Pynchon.

FREDERICK C. CREWS, Professor of English at the University of California, Berkeley, is the author of *Out of My System,* a critique of Freudian criticism; and studies of James, Hawthorne, and Forster.

MARTIN LUSCHEI is Professor of English at California Polytechnic State University in San Luis Obispo and the author of *The Sovereign Wayfarer: Walker Percy's Diagnosis of the Malaise* and a novel, *The Worst Season in Years.*

CLEANTH BROOKS, a founding father of the New Criticism, is Gray Professor of Rhetoric Emeritus, Yale University, and a member of the National Institute of Arts and Letters. His many books include *The Well-Wrought Urn, William Faulkner: The Yoknapatawpha Country,* and *Modern Poetry and the Tradition.*

JOYCE CAROL OATES, novelist, essayist, poet, is the author of over forty books. She teaches in the Creative Writing program at Princeton University. Among her best-known novels are *Wonderland; Childwold;* and *Them.*

RICHARD PINDELL publishes both fiction and criticism, and currently teaches English at the State University of New York at Binghamton.

SIMONE VAUTHIER is Professor of English at the Université des Sciences Humaines de Strasbourg. She is the author of numerous studies of Southern literature.

JEROME C. CHRISTENSEN is the author of *Coleridge's Blessed Machine of Language*. He has taught English at Purdue University and the State University of New York at Stony Brook.

DOREEN A. FOWLER is the author of *Faulkner's Changing Vision: From Outrage to Affirmation* and editor of several anthologies on Faulkner.

Bibliography

Arrington, Robert L. "The Mystery of Language." *The Sewanee Review* 84 (Fall 1976): cxxvii–cxxx.

Atkins, Anselm. "Walker Percy and the Post-Christian Search." *The Centennial Review* 12 (1968): 73–95.

Barnes, Julian. "Pantyhouse." *New Statesman* 94 (21 October 1977): 556–57.

Bigger, Charles P. "Logos and Epiphany: Walker Percy's Theology of Language." *The Southern Review*, n.s. 13 (1977): 196–206.

Blouin, Michel T. "The Novels of Walker Percy: An Attempt at Synthesis." *Xavier University Studies* 6 (1967): 29–42.

Bradbury, John. "Absurd Insurrection: The Barth-Percy Affair." *The South Atlantic Quarterly* 68 (1969): 319–29.

Bradbury, Malcolm. "New Fiction." *Punch* 244 (17 April 1963): 573–74.

Bradley, Jared W. "Walker Percy and the Search for Wisdom." *Louisiana Studies* 12 (1973): 579–90.

Brooks, Cleanth. "The Current State of American Literature." *The Southern Review*, n.s. 9 (1973): 273–87.

Broughton, Panthea Reid. "A Bottle Unopened, A Message Unread." *The Virginia Quarterly Review* 52 (Winter 1976): 155–60.

———, ed. *The Art of Walker Percy: Stratagems for Being.* Baton Rouge: Louisiana State University Press, 1979.

Bryant, Jerry H. *The Open Decision: The Contemporary American Novel and Its Intellectual Background.* New York: Free Press, 1970.

Cashin, Edward J. "History as Mores: Walker Percy's *Lancelot.*" *The Georgia Review* 31 (Winter 1977): 875–80.

Cheney, Brainard. "To Restore a Fragmented Image." *The Sewanee Review* 69 (Autumn 1961): 691–700.

———. "Secular Society as Deadly Farce." *The Sewanee Review* 75 (Spring 1967): 345–50.

Ciardi, John. "Why Is 20th Century Man So Sad?" *Chicago Tribune Book World* (29 June 1975): 6.

Coles, Robert. *Walker Percy: An American Search.* Boston: Little, Brown, 1979.

Culler, Jonathan. "Man the Symbol-Monger." *The Yale Review* 65 (Winter 1976): 261–66.

Daniel, John. "Fatality and Futility." *The Spectator* (3 May 1963): 572–73.

Daniel, Robert D. "Walker Percy's Lancelot: Secular Raving and Religious Silence." *The Southern Review*, n.s. 14 (Winter 1978): 186–94.

Davis, Hope Hale. "Escape Within Walls." *The New Leader* 60 (25 April 1977): 14–15.

Donadio, Stephen. "America, America." *Partisan Review* 33 (Summer 1966): 448–52.

Douglas, Ellen. *Walker Percy's* The Last Gentleman: *Introduction and Commentary*. New York: Seabury Press, 1969.

Dubus, Andre. "Paths to Redemption." *Harper's Magazine* 254 (April 1977): 86–88.

Gardner, John. "The Quest for the Philosophical Novel." *New York Times Book Review* (20 February 1977).

Gilman, Richard. "*The Second Coming* by Walker Percy." *The New Republic* 183 (5 & 12 July 1980): 29–31.

Godschalk, William Leigh. "Walker Percy's Christian Vision." *Louisiana Studies* 13 (1974): 130–41.

Godwin, Stephen. "After the Faulkners." *Shenandoah* 23 (Winter 1972): 70–77.

Hall, Constance. "The Ladies in *The Last Gentleman*." *Notes on Mississippi Writers* 11 (1978): 26–35.

Hicks, Granville. "One of the Roaming Kind." *Saturday Review* 49 (18 June 1966): 29–30.

Hoffman, Frederick J. *The Art of Southern Fiction: A Study of Some Modern Novelists*. Carbondale: Southern Illinois University Press, 1967.

Hyman, Stanley Edgar. "Moviegoing and Other Intimacies." *The New Leader* 45 (30 April 1962): 23–24.

Janeway, Elizabeth. "The End of the World Is Coming." *The Atlantic Monthly* 228 (August 1971): 87–90.

Johnson, Lucy. "Percy and Amis." *The Progressive* 30 (October 1966): 49–50.

Kazin, Alfred. "The Pilgrimage of Walker Percy." *Harper's Magazine* 243 (June 1971): 81–86.

———. *Bright Book of Life: American Novelists and Storytellers from Hemingway to Mailer*. Boston: Little, Brown, 1974.

Kennedy, J. Gerald. "The Semiotics of Memory: Suicide in *The Second Coming*." *Delta ES* (13 November 1981): 103–25.

Kenner, Hugh. "On Man the Sad Talker." *National Review* 27 (12 September 1975): 1000–1002.

Kissel, Susan S. "Walker Percy's 'Conversions.'" *The Southern Literary Journal* 9 (1977): 124–36.

Klein, Marcus. "Melted into Air." *The Reporter* 36 (9 February 1967): 61–62.

Kostelanetz, Richard. "The New American Fiction." In *The New American Arts*, edited by Richard Kostelanetz, 194–236. New York: Horizon Press, 1965.

Lawry, E. G. "Literature as Philosophy: *The Moviegoer*." *Monist* 63 (October 1980): 547–57.

Lawson, Lewis A. "Walker Percy as Martian Visitor." *The Southern Literary Journal* 8 (Spring 1976): 102–13.

———. "Walker Percy's Indirect Communications." *Texas Studies in Literature and Language* 11 (1969): 867–900.

———. "Walker Percy's Southern Stoic." *The Southern Literary Journal* 3 (1970): 5–31.

LeClair, Thomas. "For Walker Percy Man Is the Naming Animal." *New York Times Book Review* (8 June 1975): 6–7.

———. "The Eschatological Vision of Walker Percy." *Renascence* 26 (1974): 115–22.

Lehan, Richard. *A Dangerous Crossing: French Literary Existentialism and the Modern American Novel.* Carbondale: Southern Illinois University Press, 1973.

Locke, Richard. "Novelists as Preachers." *New York Times Book Review* (17 April 1977): 3, 52–3.

Luschei, Martin. *The Sovereign Wayfarer: Walker Percy's Diagnosis of the Malaise.* Baton Rouge: Louisiana State University Press, 1972.

Malin, Irving. "Cross Purposes." *The Virginia Quarterly Review* 53 (Summer 1977): 568–71.

Massie, Robert. "Double Features Were His Refuge." *New York Times Book Review* (28 May 1961): 30.

Maxwell, Robert. "Walker Percy's Fancy." *The Minnesota Review* 7 (1967): 231–37.

McGuane, Thomas. "This Is the Way the World Will End." *New York Times Book Review* (23 May 1971): 7, 37.

Nagel, Thomas. "Sin and Significance." *New York Review of Books* 22 (18 September 1975): 54–56.

Oates, Joyce Carol. "Gentleman Without a Past." *The Nation* 203 (8 August 1966): 129–30.

Pindell, Richard. "Basking in the Eye of the Storm: The Esthetics of Loss in Walker Percy's *The Moviegoer.*" *Boundary* 24 (1975): 219–30.

Poore, Charles. "A Candide in a Brooks Brothers Suit." *New York Times* (16 June 1966): 45.

Pritchett, V. S. "Clowns." *New York Review of Books* 16 (1 July 1971): 15.

Sheed, Wilfrid. "Ravening Particles of Anxiety." *The Critic* 25 (October–November 1967): 92–93.

———. "Additions to the Galaxy." *The National Catholic Reporter* 3 (8 February 1967): 7.

———. "The Good Word: Walker Percy Redivivus." *New York Times Book Review* (4 July 1971): 2.

Simpson, Lewis P. "The Southern Aesthetic of Memory." *Tulane Studies in English* 23 (1978): 207–27.

The Southern Quarterly 18 (Spring 1980). Special Walker Percy issue.

Sullivan, Walter. "The Insane and the Indifferent: Walker Percy and Others." *The Sewanee Review* 86 (Winter 1978): 153–59.

———. "Southerners in the City: Flannery O'Connor and Walker Percy." In *The Comic Imagination in American Literature,* edited by Louis D. Rubin, Jr., 339–48. New Brunswick, N.J.: Rutgers University Press, 1973.

———. *A Requiem for the Renascence: The State of Fiction in the Modern South.* Athens: University of Georgia Press, 1976.

Sullivan, William A. *Walker Percy.* Jackson: Mississippi Library Commission, 1977.

Tanner, Tony. *City of Words: American Fiction 1950–1970*. New York: Harper and Row, 1971.

Taylor, Lewis J., Jr. "Walker Percy and the Self." *Commonweal* 100 (10 May 1974): 233–36.

Telotte, J. P. "Walker Percy's Language of Creation." *The Southern Quarterly* 16 (1978): 105–16.

———. "Symbolic Structure for Walker Percy's Fiction." *Modern Fiction Studies* 26 (Summer 1980): 227–40.

Tenenbaum, Ruth Betsy. "Walker Percy's 'Consumer-Self' in *The Last Gentleman*." *Louisiana Studies* 15 (1976): 304–9.

Thale, Mary. "The Moviegoer in the 1950's." *Twentieth Century Literature* 14 (1968): 84–89.

Tharpe, Jac. *Walker Percy*. Boston: Twayne Publishers, 1983.

———. *Walker Percy: Art and Ethics*. Jackson: University Press of Mississippi, 1980.

Thwaite, Anthony. "Southern Pooterism." *The* (London) *Observer* (16 October 1977): 37.

Towers, Robert. "Southern Discomfort." *New York Review of Books* 24 (31 March 1977): 6–8.

Trachtenberg, Stanley. "Beyond Initiation: Some Recent Novels." *The Yale Review* 56 (Autumn 1966): 131–38.

Tyler, Anne. "The Subject is Language—With Love and Skill." *The National Observer* (19 July 1975): 21.

Van Cleave, Jim. "Versions of Percy." *The Southern Review*, n.s. 6 (1970): 990–1010.

Vauthier, Simone. "Narrative Triangle and Triple Alliance: A Look at the Movie-goer." In *Les Americanistes: New French Criticism on Modern American Fiction*, edited by Ira Johnson and Christiane Johnson, 71–93. Port Washington, N.Y.: Kennikat, 1978.

Wain, John. "The Insulted and the Injured." *New York Review of Books* (28 July 1966): 22–24.

Weber, Brom. "The Mode of 'Black Humor.'" In *The Comic Imagination in American Literature*, edited by Louis D. Rubin, Jr., 361–71. New Brunswick, N.J.: Rutgers University Press, 1973.

Weinberg, Helen. *The New Novel in America: The Kafkan Mode in Contemporary Fiction*. Ithaca, N.Y.: Cornell University Press, 1970.

Yardley, Jonathan. "Stethoscope of the Spirit." *The New Republic* 164 (22 May 1971): 25–26.

———. "The New Old Southern Novel." *Partisan Review* 40 (1973): 286–93.

Zeugner, John F. "Walker Percy and Gabriel Marcel: The Castaway and the Way-farer." *Mississippi Quarterly* 28 (1974–75): 21–53.

Acknowledgments

"*The Moviegoer* and American Fiction: Wonder and Alienation" (originally entitled "Afterword: Wonder and Alienation—The Mystic and The Moviegoer") by Tony Tanner from *The Reign of Wonder: Naivety and Reality in American Literature* by Tony Tanner, © 1965 by Cambridge University Press. Reprinted by permission of the publisher.

"The Hero as 'Case': *The Last Gentleman*" (originally entitled "The Hero as 'Case'") by Frederick C. Crews from *Commentary* 42, no. 3 (September 1966), © 1966 by The American Jewish Committee. Reprinted by permission. All rights reserved.

"The Ruins of Consensus: *Love in the Ruins*" (originally entitled "The Ruins of Consensus") by Martin Luschei from *The Sovereign Wayfarer: Walker Percy's Diagnosis of the Malaise* by Martin Luschei, © 1972 by Louisiana State University Press. Reprinted by permission of the publisher.

"Walker Percy and Modern Gnosticism" by Cleanth Brooks from *The Southern Review* 13, no. 4 (October 1977), © 1977 by Louisiana State University. Reprinted by permission of the author.

"*Lancelot*" by Joyce Carol Oates from *The New Republic* 176, no. 6 (February 5, 1977), © 1977 by *The New Republic, Inc.* Reprinted by permission.

"Toward Home: Place, Language, and Death in *The Last Gentleman*" by Richard Pindell from *The Art of Walker Percy: Stratagems for Being*, edited by Panthea Reid Broughton, © 1979 by Louisiana State University Press. Reprinted by permission of the publisher.

"Narrative Triangulation in *The Last Gentleman*" by Simone Vauthier from *The Art of Walker Percy: Stratagems for Being*, edited by Panthea Reid Broughton, © 1979 by Louisiana State University Press. Reprinted by permission of the publisher.

"*Lancelot*: Sign for the Times" by Jerome C. Christensen from *Walker Percy: Art and Ethics*, edited by Jac Tharpe, © 1980 by *The Southern Quarterly*. Reprinted by permission of the University Press of Mississippi.

"Answers and Ambiguity in Percy's *The Second Coming*" by Doreen A. Fowler from *Critique* 23, no. 2 (Winter 1981–82), © 1981 by James Dean Young. Reprinted by permission.

"Percy as Storyteller" (originally entitled "Percy as Storyteller: Or, How to Avoid Getting Zapped by the Ravening Particles") by Patricia Lewis Poteat from *Walker Percy and the Old Modern Age* by Patricia Lewis Poteat, © 1985 by Louisiana State University Press. Reprinted by permission of the publisher.

Index

Adventures of Huckleberry Finn
(Twain), 3, 12, 14
Alienation: capitalism and, 57; of child
characters, 10; in *Lancelot,* 61,
109; in *The Last Gentleman,* 74–
75; in *The Message in the Bottle,*
54; in *The Moviegoer,* 9
American ethos, 16–17, 19, 25–26
Analysis, in fiction, 16–18
Anderson, Sherwood, 9, 14, 15
Angelism-bestialism duality, 33, 45–46,
50, 59, 60, 140–43, 144
Arendt, Hannah, 127, 128
Art: defined, 14, 15–17; vs. nature, 16
Art Immelmann (*Love in the Ruins*),
34–35, 37–38, 41, 42, 45–46, 48,
49, 141, 142, 144
Assassinations, 25, 35
Atom bomb, 80
Auden, W. H., 129

Barrett, Will. *See* Will Barrett (*The
Last Gentleman*); Will Barrett
(*The Second Coming*)
Barthes, Roland, 86
Baudelaire, Charles, 17
Beckett, Samuel, 73
Bellow, Saul, 15, 18
Billy Budd (Melville), 17
Binx Bolling (*The Moviegoer*), 36, 43,
44, 63, 65, 67, 123, 128, 132–46;
faith of, 138, 139; film addiction
of, 11–12, 117; and Fitzgerald's

Carraway, vii; "Jewishness" of, 6,
10; and Melville's Ishmael, vii; as
outsider, 9–13; as quietist, 5;
"search" of, 132, 134–35, 136–
38; and Twain's Huckleberry Finn,
3
Blacks: in *Lancelot,* 66, 106, 108; in
The Last Gentleman, 22, 76, 96;
in *Love in the Ruins,* 29–30; and
Percy's satire, 140; relations with
whites of, 31–32
Blithedale Romance, The (Hawthorne),
69
Bolling, Binx. *See* Binx Bolling (*The
Moviegoer*)
Brady, Matthew, 70, 76, 99
Businessman, vs. outsider, 9

Camus, Albert, 9–10, 63
Cárdenas, García López de, 146
Castaway, image of, 136–37, 138, 145.
See also Pilgrim, man as
Catholicism, 5–6, 31, 35, 67, 140,
143; and Jews, 5; in *The Last
Gentleman,* 22–23; in *Love in the
Ruins,* 31, 44, 47, 58–59, 143; vs.
Protestant fundamentalism, 5
Central Park (New York), as metaphor,
70–73, 76, 81
"Certification" of reality, 5, 11–12
Children, nature of minds of, 10
Church: and property, 35–36; as sub-
ject of Percy's satire, 140